PRAISE FOR

Internal Family Systems Therapy for Addictions

"Addiction experts usually come in three flavors: treatment providers who tout their explicit formula for recovery, sociopolitical thinkers who understand addiction as a complex societal ill, and students of child development who recognize the trauma-strewn pathways that result in addiction and self-harm. How refreshing, then, and how remarkably comprehensive and satisfying, to see an amalgamation of all three perspectives in *Internal Family Systems Therapy for Addictions*, which then goes on to teach us precisely how to intervene.

"As a onetime addict, addiction researcher, and clinical psychologist, I'm blown away by the impact of Sykes and colleagues' IFS-guided approach to therapy. For nearly 10 years I have used this approach with my addicted clients, and there's simply nothing out there with such precision and power to help. IFS in general, and the authors' step-by-step formula for applying IFS impeccably with this difficult population, targets addiction where it lives—in the struggle between overcontrol and abandon. As these authors clarify through their singular insights and expertise, it's a struggle that gets resolved through focused attention and self-compassion, not by taking sides.

"This book is for therapists, clients, educators, coaches, and clinical researchers who've been trying to make sense of the convoluted literature and practice guidelines intended to help those who suffer from addictive disorders. It brings clarity to the chaos, both intellectually and pragmatically, but its most impressive achievement is to map out a treatment approach that actually makes a difference."

—**Marc Lewis, PhD, C.Psych,** professor emeritus (University of Toronto), clinical psychologist, and author of *The Biology of Desire: Why Addiction Is Not a Disease* and *Memoirs of an Addicted Brain*

"Until recent years, our understanding of addiction has been based on outdated and flawed assumptions—mainly that it's either a disease or a result of a lack of willpower. The IFS approach to therapy offers both a new paradigm for understanding addictive behavior through a compassionate lens and an effective framework for treating it to create lasting change. This wonderful book provides an accessible manual to therapists who are interested in tackling addictive processes at their core using IFS. *Internal Family Systems Therapy for Addictions* is a timely and important contribution that is likely to change the narrative around addiction treatment."

—**Niall McKeever,** founder of The Weekend University

"We all contain contradictions, yet when it comes to behaviors labeled as addictions, internal contradictions are often pathologized. Traditional treatment models confront the person seeking help and try to silence the 'addict' voice. Thankfully, *Internal Family Systems Therapy for Addictions* recognizes that the contradictions, including the seemingly destructive parts, must be recognized rather than suppressed.

"After more than 20 years of experience in the field, I have found very few books that escape the misguided belief that people dependent on drugs are diseased, are in denial, should be confronted, and must get specialized 'addiction treatment.' This excellent and practical book challenges and rejects that view, and even questions the term *addiction* itself.

"The authors use a logical and clear stepwise approach that does not require an expert understanding of IFS, and they include exercises for both clients and the therapist. These exercises challenge the therapist's bias and stigmatizing ideas, replacing them with an understanding of the deep struggles that people with addictive habits desperately need to reconcile. For that reason alone, this book is essential reading for any clinician working with people who use drugs addictively."

—**Shaun Shelly,** Department of Family Medicine, University of Pretoria, South Africa

"In the midst of an overdose epidemic, we are past due for novel approaches to working with those with substance use disorders, and *Internal Family Systems Therapy for Addictions* does just that. This volume provides those who might not be familiar with IFS a thorough introduction. It also offers a unique lens for both conceptualizing substance use disorders and treating them, with numerous concrete tools and practical strategies that clinicians can employ. A must-read for anyone working in addictions."

—**J. Wesley Boyd, MD, PhD,** professor of psychiatry and medical ethics, Baylor College of Medicine

"I am deeply grateful for the arrival of *Internal Family Systems Therapy for Addictions* to the healthcare literature stage. It offers a real roadmap for working with the complicated, multilayered dynamics within the 'addict' and the people surrounding them, and it illuminates a methodology for reaching the core internal pain that has been avoided or managed until it can be contacted and healed.

"The overview on addictive processes lays out with elegant clarity a thorough exploration of the addiction dynamic, a healing map, and specific, heart-led skills training and experiential exercises. The attention to the therapist role and concrete directions for addressing therapist reactivity to addictive behaviors is especially notable, as client-clinician polarities are a central challenge in addiction treatment. This book is packed with relatable human examples, all accompanied by a comprehensive treatment plan and map. Organized so that anyone can grasp the essentials and relate to the information, there are concrete tools for understanding, growth, and healing for therapists, clients, family members, members of the 12-step community, and others.

"I cannot recommend this book highly enough for all who treat, relate to, or suffer from the burden of the addiction dynamic."

—**Sarah B. Stewart, PsyD,** recognized expert in trauma, addiction, IFS, and EMDR

Internal Family Systems

Therapy for <u>Addictions</u>

Trauma-Informed, Compassion-Based Interventions for Substance Use, Eating, Gambling and More

Cece Sykes, LCSW • Martha Sweezy, PhD
Richard C. Schwartz, PhD

Published by
PESI Publishing, Inc.
3839 White Ave
Eau Claire, WI 54703

Cover: Amy Rubenzer
Editing: Jenessa Jackson, PhD
Layout: Amy Rubenzer & Alissa Schneider

ISBN: 9781683736028 (print)
ISBN: 9781683736035 (ePUB)
ISBN: 9781683736042 (ePDF)

PESI Publishing
pesipublishing.com

Dedication

This book is dedicated to my clients, for their courage and trust; to my mother, Joan, for her fierce perception; to my daughters, Hilary and Chelsea, for their love and our laughter; and to Evan, the essence of loving support.

Cece Sykes

I dedicate my efforts in this book to my stellar colleagues and former students in the psychiatry department of the Cambridge Health Alliance, long a center of learning and compassion in community mental health.

Martha Sweezy

To all of my clients who taught me to love and honor their, and my own, addict parts.

Richard C. Schwartz

About the Authors

Cece Sykes, LCSW, is a consultant and senior trainer with the Internal Family Systems Institute, where she specializes in trauma and addiction and educates therapists around the world on how to apply the IFS therapy model to addictive processes. Additionally, Sykes is now exploring how psychotherapy affects the therapist's life. She lectures, consults, and leads workshops on these and related topics, and also maintains a private practice in Chicago. She has co-authored a number of articles on treating the impact of sexual trauma in families and authored the chapter "An IFS Lens on Addiction: Compassion for Extreme Parts" in the 2017 book, *Innovations and Elaborations in Internal Family Systems Therapy.*

Martha Sweezy, PhD, is a part-time assistant professor in psychiatry at Harvard Medical School, a research and training consultant at the Center for Mindfulness and Compassion at the Cambridge Health Alliance, and a psychotherapist at a private practice in Northampton, Massachusetts. She has published articles on IFS in peer reviewed journals, co-edited two books on various applications of IFS, and co-authored three treatment manuals on IFS (on trauma, couple therapy, and now addictions), as well as the second edition of *Internal Family Systems Therapy* with Richard Schwartz. Her next book, which explores shame and guilt in the context of psychic multiplicity, will be published by Guilford Press in 2023.

Richard C. Schwartz, PhD, is the creator of Internal Family Systems, a highly effective, evidence-based therapeutic model that depathologizes the multipart personality. His IFS Institute offers training for professionals and the general public. He is currently on the faculty of Harvard Medical School, and he has published five books, including *No Bad Parts: Healing Trauma* and *Restoring Wholeness with the Internal Family Systems Model.* Dick lives with his wife, Jeanne, near Chicago, close to his three daughters and his growing number of grandchildren.

Table of Contents

Preface

The most common treatments for addiction view it as either a disease or evidence that an individual lacks willpower. Both views encourage therapists, doctors, police, courts, and the individuals who are seeking help to banish and control the active addiction part rather than getting curious about its behavior and motives. Since addiction rates are setting records every day in the United States and around the world, banishment and control efforts clearly backfire.

In this book, we propose a different treatment for addictive processes through the lens of Internal Family Systems (IFS), which flips the prevailing approach to treatment on its head. Rather than exiling their addictive part, clients are encouraged to listen to it, learn how it has been trying to protect them, and honor its efforts. At first glance, this seems dangerous and counterintuitive—why honor a disease or a compulsive, self-destructive habit that is ruining someone's body, their family, and their life?

The IFS approach only makes sense if you buy into one of its basic premises. This behavior is not evidence of a disease, nor is it the uncontrollable habit of a weak individual. It is the choice of a valuable inner being (a part), who was desperate to save the client at some point in their earlier life and, thinking it must continue to do this job or something terrible will happen, got stuck in that protective (now destructive) role. In other words, often addictive parts are desperately trying to distract or numb you from vulnerable emotions such as pain, shame, and terror, or they're trying to keep at bay other scary protectors like self-hate or suicide. Consequently, in some cases, what they are protecting must be healed or changed before it is safe for them to stop their activities.

Everyone has addictive processes. Even if you don't drink too much or use drugs in a problematic way, you do something else. Maybe you watch too much TV when you're overworking, or you eat too much when you're sad and then restrict later. Addiction signals a normal balancing act that is now too extreme.

We are well versed in the traditional approaches to addiction, and we are highly experienced IFS therapists who have worked with many forms of addictive processes. In this book we explain the differences between treatment paradigms and offer many illustrative examples. We also give clear guidelines for negotiating a ceasefire between a client's cautious, shaming, managerial protectors and their rebellious, compulsive, addictive protectors, and then we get permission to go—with the curiosity and compassion of Self—to the frightened, shocked, shamed parts who are being protected and who need to be healed.

Additionally, we include experiential exercises that aim to help you, as a therapist, get to know and appreciate your parts who become polarized around addiction—and the same exercises can be used with clients. We also introduce and illustrate an inner conference table technique, developed by Cece, which is very useful with highly enmeshed and polarized systems.

The IFS model has become very popular and influential over the past decade. At the same time, addictive processes are complicated, and we therapists are far from immune to our culture's negative beliefs about addictions, which, due to poor treatment outcomes, are commonly seen as very hard to affect. As a result, many IFS therapists continue to believe that clients who reveal an addiction should be referred to traditional treatment centers or specialized therapists. A revolution has been taking place in addictions treatment, including in some IFS-based treatment centers, and this book argues for doing things differently.

After countering the negative biases about addiction in our culture and in the field of mental health, this book invites you to take a nonshaming, depathologizing, compassionate stance toward parts who are engaged in addictive processes. If you accept this invitation and find that your clients do better when their parts feel validated, acceptable, harmonious, unburdened, and loved, we hope that you (and they) will spread the word. That message is worthy of a revolutionary movement, and we are glad to be part of it.

Acknowledgments

Cece thanks Martha for her steadfast commitment and incisive contributions every step of the way; Martha thanks Cece for her wisdom, wit, and good companionship throughout this project; and we both thank Dick for developing a systemic intrapsychic model that embraces contradiction. Dick thanks Cece for bringing her expertise on addictions to IFS and Martha for her many contributions to the IFS library. Finally, we all thank Linda Jackson, our publisher, for her patience and invaluable help, and Jenessa Jackson, our editor at PESI, for her astute help and comprehensive support.

Introduction

Addictive processes affect people's body, mind, and spirit. When people engage in compulsive, repetitive use of substances or practices like gambling, porn, high-risk sex, and over- or under-eating, it affects their physical health, reconditions their brain, and generates despair. Intimate relationships suffer, families break up, and communities fragment. Collectively, individuals who engage in addictive processes spend billions of dollars each year on alcohol, drugs, porn sites, gambling, groceries, and more. This has resulted in billions more being spent by addiction treatment centers, community mental health centers, and government systems in an attempt to address, prevent, treat, adjudicate, or incarcerate these behaviors (Hart, 2021). In psychotherapy, where do we start?

We suggest a paradigm shift. Rather than asking clients why they engage in compulsive behaviors that lead to negative consequences, we ask how these behaviors or practices help them. Rather than asking why they continue to engage in avoidant, dissociative behaviors that take them out of reality, we ask what they fear would happen if they were completely present. Rather than looking at addictive processes through the lens of mainstream treatment models, which are heavily skewed toward confronting the client and challenging their denial, we suggest engaging the client and healing attachment disruptions and other traumas that activate addictive behaviors in the first place.

We do this with a therapeutic approach called Internal Family Systems (IFS) therapy, which is based on the idea that the psyche has many parts. When one part gets hurt, other parts help by stepping into protective roles. Some protective parts have a proactive role in that they help the client to perform daily tasks and maintain social connections, while others have a reactive role, in that they distract from or soothe emotional pain. The behavior of these protective teams is very different but both have positive intentions. IFS helps clients get curious about these parts so they can discover who they are protecting and why.

When clients come to us, they are often in the grip of a short-term solution (addictive processes) to a long-term problem (disconnection and the sense of shamefulness). They feel discouraged and defeated. However, as IFS therapists, we come to this same meeting with a very different perspective. We know that all parts are deeply committed and well-intentioned. We know that compulsive parts use strategies that may have worked well for past emergencies but are much too costly in the present. We also know these parts want the client to be safe and functional. And we're confident that the options we offer are good. Instead of participating in the chronic power struggles of protective parts, we normalize internal differences, note shared goals, and guide the client to get between parts who are in conflict and help them negotiate.

In this manual, we offer a plan for treating addictive behaviors with IFS by explaining the addictive cycle, describing a series of direct interventions that engage the client without power struggles, and providing safe, clear procedures for addressing underlying emotional pain. We include many experiential exercises and detailed case examples that apply IFS to the wide range of risky behaviors clients use to navigate stress and self-medicate pain. We intend this manual to serve IFS trained therapists who feel anxious when working with addictive processes, as well as any therapist who is comfortable treating addictions but wishes to explore new options.

IFS combines systems thinking with compassionate, inner-focused, experiential psychotherapy. It places the clinician and client on the same gentle road to healing. We know that ordinary people can be loyal, loving, and successful while also being destructive to themselves and others because they're in the midst of an addictive process. The IFS model is tailor-made for that level of complexity.

SECTION I

An Overview of Internal Family Systems Therapy

THE CORE ASSUMPTIONS OF IFS

The IFS model of psychotherapy, developed by Richard Schwartz, is based on three assumptions. First, everyone has many *parts*, also known as subpersonalities, who engage with one another in their own internal community and operate much the way families and larger groups operate (Schwartz & Sweezy, 2020). Parts are normal. Having *many* parts is normal. They manifest in a developmental sequence throughout life, showing up at different ages and in different places in the body. Each part expresses its feelings and beliefs in its own way.

Second, contrary to initial appearances, the psyche's inner players are not random or unrelated. They are a system and they relate to one another in patterned ways, forming alliances and polarizing. When one part (or team of parts) becomes extreme in an effort to be safe, another part steps in to restore balance by moving in a different direction. A power struggle ensues and each side becomes more extreme, which reinforces emotional pain. In IFS, we therefore focus directly on polarizations between opposing parts as we treat clients with addictions.

Third, every person has what Schwartz calls a *Self* in addition to having parts. Schwartz landed on this word because his clients used it to describe what they felt when their parts cooperated rather than vying for control. They felt calmer, more accepting, and more spacious, and would say, "I feel more like myself now." To distinguish this concept from more mundane uses of the word, Schwartz capitalized the "S" in *Self* in his writing. In IFS, we see the Self as an undamageable inborn resource. When clients are connected with their Self, they embody qualities like curiosity, calm, courage, compassion, creativity, connection, confidence, and clarity, which Schwartz dubbed the 8 C's of Self-energy. Since a client's growing capacity to make healthy decisions is especially important in addictions treatment, this manual adds one more C to the list: choice.

EIGHT C'S OF SELF-ENERGY

Calm

Creative

Connected

Compassionate

Confident

Clarity

Courageous

Curiosity

+ Choice (9th C)

PSYCHIC MULTIPLICITY IS NOT A PATHOLOGY

In the internal family system, parts take on roles that can be divided into three distinct categories: managers, firefighters, and exiles. Managers are controlling parts who are proactive, purposeful, and future-oriented. In contrast, firefighters are reactive, impulsive, compulsive, and present-oriented. Although they act in different ways, managers and firefighters share the goal of protecting the sensitive, vulnerable parts—the exiles who can overwhelm the whole system with their emotional pain—and keeping them out of everyday consciousness.

Although these three categories of parts can be extreme, they are all integral to the psyche, and each has an indispensable role to play in our lives. The open-hearted, vulnerable exiles bring us curiosity, spontaneity, and joy; the managers make sure we function well and get things done; and the firefighters ensure that we take time to relax and have pleasure. Once the internal system trusts the Self and is willing to follow its lead, clients discover the benefit of welcoming all parts and recognize the strengths of each.

MANAGERS: PROACTIVE AND FUTURE-FOCUSED

When it comes to managers, the name says it all. This category of protectors does everything in its power to protect the system by planning ahead for any situations that could result in emotional pain. Toward this end, they promote two different goals. First, they take care of basics, like holding down a job, providing a place to live, and tending to social relationships. Second, they promote progress and personal success. For example, a striving manager might motivate a client to improve at work, get better grades, or learn new parenting skills at home. Alternatively, a judging manager might warn a client about being too angry or procrastinating too much.

Common manager behaviors include being task-oriented, rational, directive, discerning, judicious, cautious, critical, organized, analytical, serious, caretaking, concerned, thoughtful, approval-seeking, vigilant, and attentive, among others. Manager behaviors—even criticism—are designed to ensure at least a reasonable level of stability in work, living conditions, and primary relationships. In a balanced system, clients get a solid sense of confidence, satisfaction, and pride from manager-led accomplishments. Managers typically want the client to look as positive as possible: smart, likable, kind, prepared, and successful in whatever realms they choose. Since these behaviors tend to be accepted and reinforced by our larger social culture, it's easy for us to identify with most of the views of our managers.

However, some managers need to make great efforts to protect us during particularly painful moments. When clients are struggling with addictive processes, their managers are typically demanding, controlling, obsessive, and even vicious. What was once an accepted behavior in society might now be a strict order. For instance, the simple desire to do better may become a harsh demand to be flawless, and anything less than perfection is deemed worthless. These managers have no patience for mistakes and little tolerance for fear or sensitivity. Even when clients are functioning well at work and home, these parts are never satisfied. They unleash internal diatribes that fill the client with contempt, moralizing, and blame. On the whole, their intentions are positive, but their behavior tops off an inner reservoir of shamefulness and mobilizes reactive firefighter parts, who are always prepared to bring relief with substances or other options.

COMMON BEHAVIORS OF MANAGER PARTS IN ADDICTIVE SYSTEMS

- **Blaming critic:** Attacks firefighters with hostility and contempt

- **Shaming judge:** Evaluates firefighter behaviors as immoral or bad

- **Perfectionist:** Is terrified of mistakes and assumes only one way is correct

- **Logical rationalist:** Analyzes what to do by considering facts, not emotions

- **Intellectual:** Prefers talking about problems instead of taking action

- **Striver:** Is highly competitive and demanding with self and others

- **Rescuer:** Prevents other people from experiencing the natural consequences of their risk-taking behavior

- **Fixer:** Assumes personal responsibility for other people's actions or problems

- **Caretaker:** Has excessive concern about other people's feelings

- **Over-giver:** Is generous to a fault and struggles with boundaries

- **Know-it-all:** Is always right and wants things done their way

- **Controller:** Attacks firefighters and anyone else who doesn't conform to norms

COMMON MANAGER CHARACTERISTICS IN ADDICTIVE SYSTEMS

- They are responsible, compulsive workers who get tasks completed and value being productive and good. (The part may say: *This is the real me.*)

- They care about appearances and make efforts to seem legitimate, valuable, and normal.

- They are chronically anxious and vigilant. They can't relax or trust anyone— not the Self, firefighters, nor exiles—so they are very self-reliant.

- They work overtime to prevent exiles and firefighters from taking over by engaging in hostile, shaming, and blaming behavior.

- They operate from the neck up and minimize or dismiss feelings.

COMMON MANAGER FEARS

- Fear of the chaos and unpredictability created when firefighters are in action

- Fear that feelings of shame and worthlessness will flood the internal system, especially after firefighter activity

- Fear that the Self is not strong enough to help firefighters, often doubting that the Self exists

- Fear that secrets, old memories, and painful emotional wounds will be exposed and reinjured

- Fear that nothing will change, that firefighters cannot change their behavior, and that the underlying isolation, grief, and shame cannot be healed

FIREFIGHTERS: REACTIVE AND PRESENT-FOCUSED

The firefighters in your town or city are brave, committed, and ready for action. They do whatever it takes to save others, including risking their own lives. This is the image Schwartz had in mind when he labeled the second category of protectors. Also known as distractors or soothers, firefighter parts are reactive. They leap into action when the emotional pain of feeling worthless and unlovable breaks into consciousness, doing whatever it takes to distract the mind and soothe the body.

Some firefighter behaviors tend to be viewed as more socially acceptable. These include snacking, eating sweets, having a few drinks, eating cannabis edibles, taking sleep medications, engaging in screen time, exercising, shopping, daydreaming, reading, sleeping, flirting, playing video games, and pursuing adventurous sports. However, more extreme firefighter behaviors can include high-risk alcohol or drug use, disordered eating, self-injury, a chronic preoccupation with pornography, high-risk gambling, violence, and so on. Sometimes it takes more than one activity to soothe emotional pain, so a variety of firefighters get going at the same time. For example, an individual may combine alcohol or drug use with gambling and high-risk sexual practices. When these short-term solutions continue unabated, they accrue long-term costs, but firefighter parts are only concerned with immediate relief.

While firefighters are the agents of avoidance, they also provide hidden pleasures. These pleasures are not new. Historically, humans have always engaged in stimulating, relaxing, mood-altering, and transcendent practices. Pottery jars found in northern China that date from 7000 to 6600 BC provide early evidence of humans brewing alcohol. Ancient Sumerians in 3400 BC referred to the red poppy flower as the "joy plant." Early evidence of cannabis and peyote date back at least 2,500 years. Gambling originated during the Paleolithic period, before written history, and the earliest six-sided pair of dice date to around 3000 BC in Mesopotamia. The pursuit of sexual pleasure is, of course, ubiquitous, although conventions about when, with whom, and how to be sexual have always varied widely.

In this way, firefighter parts have always played a vital role in our lives. In a balanced system, where they don't need to spend every waking hour distracting from or soothing wounded parts, they can deploy their spontaneous, lively energy for other pursuits. In better circumstances, they counterbalance the drive of managers in good ways by shifting gears, changing the scenery, and promoting rest, relaxation, pleasure, fun, and novelty (Sykes, 2016). They offset the managerial focus on accomplishment with sensuous experiences—eating chocolate, enjoying the swig of a cold drink, racing downhill on a mountain bike, or napping on a still afternoon. When we listen closely to their intentions, even firefighters who are trapped in extreme roles want us to have pleasure, rest, and a change of perspective. They add spice and adventure as well rest and renewal to the humdrum security of a routine life.

COMMON BEHAVIORS OF FIREFIGHTER PARTS IN ADDICTIVE SYSTEMS

- Alcohol use

- Prescription or street drug use

- Disordered eating (bingeing, purging, comfort eating, or restricting)

- Gambling and overspending

- Sexual preoccupation, chronic sexual fantasizing, or sexual risk-taking

- Self-harm (cutting, head banging, etc.)

- Suicidal ideation or attempts

- Rage, violence, exploitation, or abuse of others

- Dissociating, tuning out, getting "lost," or lacking awareness of the present

- Fantasizing about idealized images of success, power, or perfect relationships

COMMON FIREFIGHTER CHARACTERISTICS IN ADDICTIVE SYSTEMS

- They are chaotic, out of control, and driven to keep using.

- They are both impulsive (unthinking and unconcerned about consequences) and compulsive (have no sense of choice).

- They are complex—can be either soothing or distracting in ways that are grossly overstimulating.

- They are heroic in that they don't back down, even under fire; they will take a bullet for the system.

- They are narcissistic, self-absorbed, and concerned primarily with the emotions and unmet needs of certain parts in the client's system.

- They are resistant to feedback and will avoid noticing or listening to the impact of their behavior on the client and others. In turn, they will also deny, hide evidence, and minimize (by lying) about how much the client is using.

- They are committed and will stay on the job until they're convinced that exiles are safe enough.

COMMON FIREFIGHTER FEARS

- Fear that the hopelessness and despair of exiles will flood the system and cause a functional collapse

- Fear that managers will be exhaustingly shaming and inhibiting, and that they may evoke a suicidal part

- Fear that managers will accommodate other people too much

- Fear that the therapist, manager parts, family members, partners, and so on will control the client in detrimental ways

- Fear that their role as essential protectors will be underestimated

- Fear that they will be misunderstood

EXILES: EMOTIONALLY OVERWHELMING AND PAST-ORIENTED

Exiles, the third category of parts, are the young, sensitive, and most vulnerable parts of the inner system. When nurtured and protected, they embody innocence, trust in others, and open-heartedness. However, their dependence on others for nurture makes these tender parts vulnerable to wounding. They are quick to interpret the insult of neglect, or the pain of sexual, physical, or emotional transgressions, as information about their own inherent value. As a result, they feel lonely and become burdened with the belief that they are worthless, weak, undeserving, unlovable, or bad. Managers and firefighters fear these beliefs and feelings, and they work overtime to banish exiles—and their unintegrated memories and unhealed attachment wounds—from awareness. The extent to which protectors expend their energy on this work is proportional to the exile's wounding. The more severe the wound, the more energy protectors put into their job.

Simply having exiles does not necessarily mean our parents or caretakers were inattentive, careless, or negligent—no one can be perfectly attuned and available at all times. For this reason, we all have some wounded, exiled parts—and protectors to defend these parts. But the less supportive the environment, the greater the injury, and the more protectors feel obliged to exile injured parts. For example, children who were alienated from their family or community (e.g., a transgender or gay child in a transphobic, homophobic environment), who experienced significant loss (e.g., the death of a parent), who were neglected (e.g., lack or food, medical care, dental care, or housing), who were treated harshly (e.g., verbally, physically, or sexually assaulted), or who were exploited (e.g., made to provide primary care for siblings) are likely to develop extreme protectors at an early age. In fact, clients who grew up in rough circumstances often report having been drawn to shoplifting, smoking cigarettes, or eating for comfort by the age of six or eight. These were their first firefighter activities. The more alarming their situation, the harder their protectors worked to exile feelings that threatened to flood them and paralyze their internal systems.

This is only sensible. Who would not seek relief from a prolonged onslaught of emotional pain? When children aren't protected externally, they fashion internal protection from the tools at hand. This notion is borne out by the Adverse Childhood Experiences (ACE) study, which found that childhood trauma is associated with a variety of adverse health outcomes later in life (Felitti et al., 1998). The ACE study showed that people who were exposed to early trauma were likely to develop firefighter parts who self-medicated with nicotine, alcohol, drugs, comfort food—all while their manager parts were holding down jobs and trying to function.

In our view, it's never too late to heal wounded parts, even for clients who have gotten trapped in high-risk lifestyles that accrued big costs. Exiles may carry the great burden of a denigrated identity, but their natural state is the trusting, open-hearted, and playful nature of any well-nurtured baby or young child. When we honor and protect the vulnerability of these parts, we can help clients maintain access to a sense of wonder, joy, and lightheartedness. We can help them be carefree, open to new experiences, and sensitive to others without feeling overwhelmed or responsible for their troubles.

If IFS, we guide clients to rediscover their Self and release the exiles who were burdened with unbearable beliefs, like *I am too much* or *I am not enough.* We help them recognize that these beliefs are not factual information; they are a product of experience. For some, this is a long road filled with starts and stops. Yet the art of preventing the recurrence of addictive behaviors is the art of connecting with exiles safely, and this art is teachable.

The System: A Balancing Act[*]

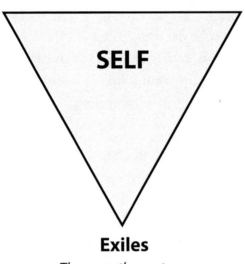

Managers

These are the parts we overidentify with

- Attempt to stabilize or improve the system
- Are future-oriented
- Are proactive

SELF

Firefighters

These are the parts we reject or conceal

- Soothe or distract from emotional pain
- Are present-oriented
- Are reactive

Exiles

These are the parts we repress or ignore

- Absorb energy
- Are past-oriented
- Are overwhelming

SELF IS THE HEART OF THE MATTER

As we've discussed, the Self is our seat of kind awareness and wakeful presence. It is a compassionate, nonjudgmental witness to our experiences, inside and out. It is an inner place of knowing that can be obscured by the activities of parts but, like the sun, is always present and available when stormy weather clears. As clients embody their Self over the course of therapy, their awareness broadens to encompass both the external relational field and the inner landscape.

When we listen to a client's chaotic stories of self-destruction, we may wonder, *Does this person have a Self?* It's a good question. A client who regularly uses substances or engages in other addictive practices may have very little access to moments of insight or confidence. But their Self-energy does show up in more subtle ways, and an IFS therapist understands that all clients have the capacity to access their Self from the beginning of therapy, even if for only a few moments at a time. For example, the Self may appear in the simple wish for a less-fraught life, the urgent longing to be a better parent, or the desire to

---

* Adapted with permission from "An IFS Lens on Addiction: Compassion for Extreme Parts," by C. Sykes, in M. Sweezy & E. L. Ziskind (Eds.), *Innovations and Elaborations in Internal Family Systems Therapy* (p. 30), 2017, Routledge (https://doi.org/10.4324/9781315775784). Copyright 2017 by Cece Sykes, LCSW.

feel better when they wake up in the morning. Clients may also report hearing a wise inner voice when they're high or in an altered state of mind. It might warn them of danger, tell them to go home, or remind them to look after a friend.

During the course of therapy, we need to build on these small moments of clarity. We focus on identifying and dispersing the client's activated parts so they can experience at least a measure of inner calm, quiet, wisdom, and warmth. It can sometimes feel like we're moving at a snail's pace, moving forward only a centimeter or two at a time! Yet when parts get noticed and have the chance to connect with the Self, they loosen up, and this benefits the rest of the system. Critically, these new Self-to-part connections offer the client many moments of choice, each of which is an opportunity to try new behaviors.

BASIC CONCEPTS FOR THE CLINICAL APPLICATION OF IFS

Blending

To practice IFS, you must understand the concept of *blending*. When a client feels engulfed by a particular feeling or speaks from the perspective of just one part, we say that this part is *blended*. For example, let's say that a client drinks every day but declares, "There's no way my drinking is hurting anything!" The IFS therapist hears this as a firefighter part who loves or feels a need to drink. This part has strong feelings and a big impact, but it does not represent the client's best judgment or their system's majority view.

Similarly, let's say a client is struggling with binge eating and is despondent about their nightly eating pattern. They exclaim with disgust, "I'm terrible—this can't go on. I have to stop!" Here, the client is dismayed about eating compulsively but not curious about the function of the eating, which tells the IFS therapist that the client is blended with a judgmental manager as opposed to being connected with their Self.

Unblending

Parts can show up in one of three ways. First, they may appear as thoughts or ideas. For example, a client may think, *I now see that this job is not a good fit for me anymore.* Second, they can show up as a physical sensation or an urge. A client may experience a rapid heartbeat, a desire to get away, or a craving to eat, get high, gamble, or watch porn. Third, parts can manifest as a feeling or mood. For example, a client may say, "I've been worried all day" or "I feel so sad about my son." Since clients are usually not aware of blended parts—but, rather, identify with them—the therapist's primary role in IFS is to be a "parts detector" and guide the client in helping the part to unblend.

Toward that end, we help clients notice their parts, and then we guide them to persuade a target part th[at] it would benefit by unblending. The therapist might say, "It sounds like we're hearing from a part who is really invested in drinking and can't see any problems. Is that right?" or "It sounds lik[e] one very critical part who is worried about the nighttime eating. Do you hear that part?" [Once] able to tune in to the part, the therapist can help them interview it about its intention[s]

Sometimes, clients are blended with several parts serially, so they float from one thought, feeling, or urge to the next—and these can be contradictory. For example, a client might begin a session with several parts pouring their hearts out: "I think I need to quit my job. It's not working for me anymore. I wanted to run out of there all week, but I can't afford to. And I'm so worried about what's happening with my daughter when I'm not at the house. I shouldn't have had so much to drink last night, but I can't sleep anymore, and then this morning I overslept and showed up late!"

When parts fight for center stage within consciousness, emotions mix and thoughts brawl. But whether one part is in the spotlight or several switch in and out, our goal is to make room for the client's Self, which happens when all their parts are willing to unblend. To that end, we ask the client to pick *one* target part, no matter how many parts the client describes at first. Then we ask, "How do you feel toward _____ [*the target part*]?" Their answer reveals either the presence of other blended parts or, if all parts have unblended, the presence of the client's Self.

If one part will not unblend, or many parts are blending in a serial fashion, we point out their conflict—for example, how one part wants to leave a certain job and another doesn't, or how one part wants to drink at night and another doesn't—and offer to help both sides. We ask if these parts would all be willing to unblend at least long enough to accept one moment of kindness and attention from the client's Self. Once they get connected in that way, we can ask which part needs the client's attention first. Just a few moments of everyone noticing each other can be revelatory and counts as unblending practice, with an aim of helping all parts unblend over time. When parts unblend, the client can see them more clearly, understand their desire for relief, and offer to help.

The Mini-Unblend for Quick Calming

Clients with addictive processes often show up for sessions feeling overwhelmed. Their emotions are running high, one chaotic story is spilling into another, and they are hungry for attention and care. This blast is likely to rouse the therapist's own managers, who want order, yet we also know that an abrupt push for clients' unblending may be received as unempathetic and dismissive. As a result, it's good to have another strategy for calming clients and slowing their systems down.

We recommend a *mini-unblend* (pause, breathe, notice), which welcomes the client's whole system, just as it is right now. Here's how to do it: We start with attuned, concerned listening and no agenda. We let the client spill ... tion they need to. If it feels right, we make a mirroring statement or two, ... fter a short while, we validate how hard the client has been trying, notice ... eek, or acknowledge all they had to do just to get here, and then suggest ... en the client calms, we can speak with the blended part directly, or the ... r inquiry.

... ialogue and a lot of guesswork. The client reports on their week, the ... tful questions, the client responds, they ponder motives together, and ... client guess about their motives (*Maybe you binged because you were* ... tly move to nonjudgmental curiosity (*Let's find the part who binged*

last night and ask why). If the bingeing part says it behaved this way because it didn't want the client to be angry, we understand the behavioral sequence, and we can then help the client build relationships with both the bingeing part and the angry part—and we can move toward learning whom they protect. In this way, the client repeatedly discovers that protective parts shield vulnerable parts, which naturally leads to the key question, *Would you need to act this way if we could help the vulnerable part?*

We conduct nonjudgmental inquiries by starting with a chain of six questions—which we call the 6 F's—and continue on from there with more questions.

Clients are generally surprised and pleased when their parts talk back (or somehow communicate with them) in response to these questions. Hearing directly from their parts about their fears and their disagreements with each other helps the client make sense of subjective experiences that otherwise seem chaotic, confusing, and nonsensical. This, alone, can be a great relief. Since parts are less likely to judge what they understand, critical managers may also calm down or unblend more easily when they listen to the client interview reactive firefighters. Every little step on this inner journey moves in the direction of parts cooperating with each other and trusting the client's Self.

THE 6 F'S

1. **Find** a part: Who needs your attention today?

2. **Focus** on the part: How does it show up? What kind of energy does it have? Where do you notice it in or around your body?

3. How do you **feel** toward the part? Accepting, judgmental, or neutral? When you notice this part, do you feel open and curious, guarded and cautious, angry and rejecting, or something else?

4. **Flesh** out the part's role: What are its original intentions for the internal system? What are its signature behaviors? How long has it been in this role? Who is it protecting?

5. Be**friend** the part: How does it respond to you? What would it need to trust the connection with you?

   - If the part feels safe enough with the client to share without reservation, we can be confident that the client's Self is present. But if a protector is criticizing the target part or doesn't want to listen to it, we know a critical manager is present, and we ask it to unblend. If it refuses, it becomes our target part.

6. Discover the part's **fears**. What would other protectors do if this one stopped its behavior? Has that scenario played out in the past? What would happen to the hurt, exiled parts if it stopped this behavior? Has that ever happened in the past?

Getting to Know a Manager

Managers are proactive and future-oriented parts who want you to improve and make progress. Toward this end, they may engage in a variety of behaviors like perfectionism, self-criticism, analyzing, approval-seeking, planning, striving, minimizing, controlling, moralizing, and overworking. This exercise guides you to befriend a manager part whose activity feels familiar to you. Choose any part who would like your attention; it doesn't need to be extreme.

1. First, get comfortable. There is no right way to do this exercise. Just follow your breath to your inner world, and when you're ready, ask for a manager part who would like some attention.

2. Once you've identified a manager, place that part on the other side of a one-way mirror. Invite it to be active and do what it usually does while you observe. Notice its body language and facial expressions. Listen to what it says. For example, you may begin to observe a part who is always planning: when to shop for groceries, what time to retrieve the children, when to walk the dog, how to fit in extra tasks, how to complete a work project, and so on. Tell that part that you're right there watching and you want to know more. If you don't see the part because it's more auditory than physical—for example, a perfectionist part who shows up as a voice in your mind or as a buzzing pressure near your head—you can still let it know that you're listening or feeling its energy and you're open to its message.

3. If at any point another part activates, ask it to relax and offer to check on it later, then return to the manager who is your target part. Whenever reactive parts emerge in this manner, ask them to relax. When you feel open and curious, return to the target manager and resume listening. Notice how you feel toward this manager, and if you're still feeling curious, here are some questions to ask:

   - When you pressure me to _____ [*fill in the blank with the manager's usual behavior, such as planning ahead, making no mistakes, making sure my supervisor is happy, etc.*], how are you trying to help?

   - How long have you been helping me this way?

   - How old are you?

   - Do you remember a time when acting like this became especially important? What was going on then?

- Was there ever a time when you couldn't help me to act this way? If so, what was that like for you and what happened?

- What are you afraid would happen if you took a break or stopped doing what you do? How long have you had these fears and concerns?

- Have you ever been in a situation where these fears actually came true?

- Have you ever tried to take a break from doing what you do? What happened then? How did you return to your role and get things back on track?

- When you look at me, whom do you see? (Sometimes the part sees another part. For example, it might see you as an eight-year-old child or as an acting-out firefighter part.)

- What else do you want me to know about you?

As you ask these questions, you might find that some manager parts use language to talk back to you, as if you are conversing. Other parts communicate nonverbally by showing you images to answer your questions or explain their motivations without using words. Whatever communication you get from the part, check to see if your heart is open. If so, let it know that you're paying attention and that you understand what it's telling you. If you don't understand, ask it to clarify. Some people find it helpful to respond to the part with words like, "Now that makes sense to me. I get why you want to be sure I don't fail. I appreciate your hard work."

When you understand the part's intentions and fears, thank it for sharing and acknowledge its hard work. Let it know that you want to stay in touch and help out so it's not alone. If it doesn't seem to know or trust you, acknowledge that this can easily be the case because relationships take time; let it know that you're prepared to be patient. Finally, notice how the part responds to your support, offer to stay connected, and take notes for future reference.

Getting to Know a Firefighter

Firefighters are protectors who react to manager overreach and to the surfacing of exiled pain. The most common firefighter activities involve self-medicating with alcohol, drugs, food, or sexual practices, including looking at pornography. Other firefighter parts also use gambling, shopping, screen time, exercise, physical violence, and self-harm behaviors, to name a few. Many people combine firefighter options (e.g., drinking and engaging in unprotected sex). However, this exercise guides you to befriend *one* firefighter part whose activity feels familiar. The part's behavior doesn't need to be extreme, and it can be a former behavior, like smoking in high school.

1. First, get comfortable. There is no right way to do this exercise. Just follow your breath inside, and when you're ready, ask who would like your attention.

2. Once you've identified a firefighter, place that part on the far side of a one-way mirror and invite it to be active and do what it usually does while you observe. Notice its body language and facial expressions. Is it happy and relaxed? Tense and over-stimulated? Drowsy and checked out?

3. How do you feel as you watch this part engage in its usual practice? If you notice judgment, fear, or embarrassment coming up, ask those parts to step back and offer to check on them later. Tell them that you (the Self) are merely connecting with this part, not encouraging or endorsing its behaviors. When you feel open and curious, return to the target firefighter part and ask these questions:

   - When you pressure me to _____ [*fill in the blank with the firefighter's usual behavior, such as having a few beers or bingeing on late-night movies*], how are you trying to help?

   - How long have you been helping me this way?

   - How old are you?

   - Do you remember a time when acting like this became especially important? What was going on then?

   - Was there ever a time when you couldn't help me by acting this way? If so, what was that like for you and what happened?

- What are you afraid would happen if you took a break or stopped doing what you do? How long have you had these fears and concerns?

- Have you ever been in a situation where these fears actually came true?

- Have you ever tried to take a break from doing what you do? What happened then? How did you return to your role?

- When you look at me, whom do you see? (Sometimes the part sees another part. For example, it might see you as an eight-year-old child, or as a critical manager.)

- What else do you want me to know about you?

As you ask these questions, you might find that some firefighter parts use language to talk back to you, as if you are conversing. Other parts communicate nonverbally by showing you images to answer your questions or explain their motivations without using words. Whatever communication you get from the part, check to see if your heart is open. If so, let it know that you're paying attention and that you understand what it's telling you. If you don't understand, ask it to clarify. Some people find it helpful to respond to the part with words like, "Now that makes sense to me. I get why you want to numb me from these painful emotions. I appreciate your hard work."

When you understand the part's intentions and fears, thank it for sharing and acknowledge its hard work. Let it know that you want to stay in touch and help out so it's not alone. If it doesn't seem to know or trust you, acknowledge that this can easily be the case because relationships take time; let it know that you're prepared to be patient. Finally, notice how the part responds to your support, offer to stay connected, and take notes for future reference.

Direct Access and In-Sight

Clients will nearly always arrive to their first appointment blended with a part. If they are concerned and hopeful, they're blended with a manager who convinced them to try therapy. If they're wary, hostile, paranoid, or accusing, they're blended with a firefighter. If they're hopeless and tearful, they're blended with an exile. We start by interviewing the blended part directly, and we have a couple of choices about how to do that:

1. The first choice is to act as if we're speaking with the client, not just a part of the client, even though we know we are speaking with a part. In this case, we use the pronoun *you*—what do *you* notice, what do *you* feel, what brings *you* here, and so on. This sounds just like traditional talk therapy, and we call it *implicit direct access*.

2. The second choice is to name the part as a part and talk with it about the client. In this case, we use the client's preferred pronouns to talk about them in the third person. We call this *explicit direct access*. We might say, for example, "So you are the part of Mark who is concerned about his cocaine use. Is that right?"

Once we speak directly with one or more of the client's blended parts using direct access, we then ask the part to unblend. If it won't unblend, we assume it has a good reason and we keep using direct access to learn more. But if it will unblend, the client's Self shows up and the internal Self-to-part attachments we are looking for begin to crystallize. At this point, it's best for the client's Self to take over and communicate directly with the client's parts, which is known as *in-sight*. If the client has steady access to their Self, the therapist can just step back and ask, "What needs to happen next?" But if the client's access to the Self is sketchy, the therapist can keep offering guidance as needed. As illustrated in examples throughout this manual, both in-sight and direct access are effective, though direct access can be particularly useful with polarized parts. Use both strategies liberally across sessions and clients.

What If?

Once proactive (manager) and reactive (firefighter) teams notice the client's Self and understand that they share the goal of protecting injured parts, we can suggest a new way forward by asking the following series of *what-if* questions. Our vision is hopeful (*There is an easier way!*), and protectors are typically intrigued by optimistic hypotheticals.

HYPOTHETICAL WHAT-IFS TO HELP A PART UNBLEND

- What if there was another way to handle this vulnerability?

- What if there was an effective way out of this chaotic, addictive cycle?

- What if isolated, wounded parts could heal in relationship with the Self?

- What if we could help the firefighters so they didn't have to handle the vulnerable parts all alone?

- What if we could help the managers so they didn't have to shoulder all the responsibility by themselves?

- What if you had support?

After the client has reflected on one or more of these what-ifs, ask them to pose the following question to their manager and firefighter teams: Would you be open to taking a break if you saw the Self helping these vulnerable parts?

SECTION II
Conceptualizing Addiction

ATTACHMENT WOUNDS, TRAUMA, AND THE ADDICTIVE SYSTEM

When children can bask in the warmth of stable, affectionate, and attentive caregivers, they feel safe and learn to trust themselves and others as they venture out into the world. They trust that they can express all their feelings, including silliness, grief, anger, and more. Kids who are secure and safe also feel joy and delight in the power and energy of their body—they touch everything in sight; strengthen their muscles through play; splash in bathtubs; move through the world on scooters, bicycles, and bare feet; and tenderly reach for the hand of a younger sibling or a friend.

In the ideal childhood, kids know that they're free to make mistakes and miss the mark as they learn. They know help is nearby if consequences arise and they will receive gentle guidance when they need to make a repair. Their caregivers protect them from the dangerous conditions and people they meet along the way. Their system and the system around them are in balance. Their managers discover the joy, pride, and satisfaction of accomplishment and growth. Their firefighters develop pleasurable, healthy activities that allow them to relax and pursue new adventures. Their vulnerable parts are open-hearted, loving, and receptive to love. They feel secure, loved, and free to be fully embodied. They can flourish.

However, life is rarely ideal. Obstacles pop up along the way. While emotional and physical pain are part of life, many clients with addictive behaviors have experienced more pain than they could bear. Some clients grew up in the midst of excruciating family dynamics, exploited or neglected by adults who they feared and reviled but also longed for and sometimes—confoundingly—loved. Since young children read their emotions as important information about *themselves*, not about others in their environment, those who experience neglect or abuse are especially likely to feel personally responsible for their caretaker's behavior.

But clients can grow up in more stable environments and, still, for one reason or another, develop burdensome beliefs about their value and lovability. Some clients may struggle as a result of their temperament or a specific learning disability. Others get thrown off balance by painful relationship ruptures later in life, or they collapse when connections fracture due to a divorce or an untimely death. Still others have physical challenges or chronic illness to contend with. All of these kinds of experiences can burden vulnerable parts and summon protectors who offer relief. Life is wounding, and a person may engage in compulsive practices at some point along the way for innumerable reasons. Whatever the cause, IFS therapists build a collaborative, nonjudgmental connection that helps clients heal their wounded parts and free their protectors.

THE SOCIAL CONTEXT OF ADDICTION: POLARIZATIONS WRIT LARGE

Not only does the family system deeply affect the development of a child's inner system, but the family system also nests within larger social systems that are profoundly influential. This includes systems at the neighborhood and community level, such as schools and religious organizations, as well as local, state, and federal government systems. These systems often contain a variety of polarizations that exacerbate the tension between managers and firefighters and contribute to a social context that exacerbates addiction. This is particularly the case in American culture and its institutions, which contain numerous polarities that illustrate the tension between constraint and compulsive disinhibition, between harsh moralizing and encouraged indulgence.

The economy in the United States, for example, is built on compulsive conspicuous consumption, yet compulsive practices are viewed as a moral failing. Religious and governing institutions police sexuality, female bodies, and sexual preferences while mainstream advertising sexualizes just about everything, making especially liberal use of the female body. Some psychoactive substances are banned and vilified, while others—with equal or greater potential for destructive use—are legal. Similarly, corporations market unhealthy, fattening foods and fight to keep them placed in schools for children, while the mainstream media celebrates anorexic bodies and sermonizes that thinner is better. Manager parts absorb and adopt these confusingly contradictory views at an early age—in the family, at school, in places of worship, in the media, and in an individual's interface with government institutions.

The polarity between inhibition and disinhibition is writ particularly large in the so-called war on drugs. Here, we find a strong and steady appetite for substance use across all demographic groups (Hart, 2021), which contrasts sharply with draconian government prohibitions that were designed to systematically disenfranchise Black, Indigenous, Latinx, and Asian communities, as well as other immigrants and people of color, for drug use (Hari, 2015; Hart, 2021). Government institutions have historically attacked recreational drug use among Black males and incarcerated them at five times the rate of their White counterparts, who were using recreational drugs at very similar rates. In the same context, pharmaceutical companies have, in recent years, made enormous profits by openly pedaling patently false information about prescribed opiates, leading to about 50,000 yearly overdose deaths in the United States by 2019.

And this is only a small part of the picture. We see this epidemic of addiction-related deaths in the context of larger epidemics that relate to disinhibition. Each year in the United States, while approximately 95,000 people die alcohol-related deaths and more than 100,000 die drug-related deaths, an additional 300,000 die from various causes related to obesity, and 480,000 die from the use of tobacco. However, millions of people eat, drink alcohol, gamble occasionally, or use drugs recreationally without causing themselves any major difficulties (Hart, 2021). The fatalities that result from compulsive practices are primarily, in our view, evidence of unaddressed suffering. This suffering can arise from large-scale issues (like institutional racism, patriarchy, and the entrenched materialism of a consumer-based economy) or personal histories of trauma and loss (Felitti, 2004; Hari, 2015; Menakem, 2017; Szalavitz, 2016; Schwartz & Sweezy, 2020).

Although individual psychotherapy can certainly not overhaul social ills, we continue to work to repair the individual lives of our clients. If a client lives in dangerous circumstances or engages in criminalized activities, we can guide them to hear the stories of their firefighter parts and the impact of their childhood environment. If their circumstances at home are dangerous, we can validate their reality and help them access services and reclaim parts they have exiled for personal, social, or political reasons. Validation is an antidote to shaming experiences and the remedy for internalized mistreatment, but it can't only emanate from us. A client must get validation from *within* by detaching from critical protectors, listening to their intentions with compassion and understanding, and offering a safe refuge to wounded parts.

POLARIZATIONS BETWEEN PROTECTORS

Given the various polarities we see at play in the context of the family and larger social systems, it should come as no surprise that polarizations between protective parts are the norm in addictive processes. These oppositions form when managers and firefighters devote themselves to contrasting strategies of protecting an internal system that is chronically threatened by exposure to frightening memories and painful feelings. Both teams of protectors are constantly striving to keep the system from being overwhelmed by exiled parts. While manager parts help the client function, firefighter parts use substances and other forms of soothing or distraction to keep the feelings of exiles at bay. Alone, untended, and often denigrated as too weak or too innocent, exiles get caught in the crossfire. Their unmet needs escalate, they feel ever more hopeless, and so it goes, sometimes for years, before the individual seeks or gets access to therapy.

The Polarization Cycle

1. Fragile, underlying exiles who feel deficient, inadequate, and abandoned—for any number of reasons, both historical and present-day—activate due to external interactions or challenges in the client's life.

2. Managers ignore or try to contain these vulnerable parts by getting busy, concentrating on tasks or the needs of others, keeping the client in their head, or using criticism to goad the exile into improving and becoming acceptable.

3. Noting the exile's distress and shamefulness, firefighters take over, using substances and various practices (*whatever it takes!*) to mask or medicate emotional pain.

4. Exiles feel sick, degraded, fearful, and isolated.

5. Managers mobilize again:

   a. Task managers frantically mobilize to get operations back on track in hopes of regaining fleeting control and self-respect.

   b. Critical, moralizing managers attack, vilify, and shame firefighters for their repeated transgressions.

6. Firefighters return to the addictive practice again (*something, anything!*) to further medicate the pain, block out the shame, and deny consequences.

7. Vulnerable exiles, unsought and unwanted, feel abandoned again, which reinforces their sense of being hopeless and unlovable. The cycle continues.

Since all of this occurs in a cycle, we prefer the term *addictive process* instead of *addiction*. Referring to addiction as a process also implies the developmental aspects of compulsive using, since in a chaotic environment, the addictive process can begin early (Lewis, 2015; Szalavitz, 2016). Here, a child may oscillate between manager parts who crave control and good behavior and firefighter parts who crave diversion, escape, and pain relief. For example, a child who feels compelled to take care of the wayward adults in their life might vacillate between a part who excels at sports and a part who is always dieting. They may fluctuate between a part who strives for perfect grades and a part who smokes cigarettes and shoplifts. These activities distract from, but do not help, the child's deprived young parts who need parenting. As exiles feel more desperate and the child's firefighter team gets angrier, more desperate, and more extreme, the balance between inhibition and disinhibition becomes ever more precarious. This is an addictive process.

When a client's vulnerable parts have not been as deeply wounded, the inner dynamic is milder but still present. They may wind up feeling a little stuck, a little unsuccessful. The client may not be as patient as they'd like with their partners or kids. In turn, their firefighters go to work to distract and soothe. They spend too much time lying around playing video games or scrolling through social media. Meanwhile, their managers nag and scold these screen-loving, couch-potato firefighter parts to close that laptop, get off the sofa, and be a little nicer today! This is not a major inner battle, but it is a polarity.

Polarities escalate in response to emotional pain that stems from an accumulation of negative experiences that harsh managers echo internally. Some clients report a long developmental trajectory for their addictive process and have had treatment before. Some arrive at therapy for the first time, feeling spurred to action by some threat, like job loss, after many years of trying to control their addictive process. In contrast, some clients report that an addictive behavior only became a problem after a recent stressor. Widowed seniors, for example, may start gambling away their homes and pension checks after losing their partner, illustrating a very recent need for relief from isolation and grief.

Once the addictive process (*I have to do it! I have to stop doing it!*) becomes extreme and chronic, it can't be resolved with simple negotiation. The antipathy and lack of trust between the two sides runs too deep. Therefore, rather than soliciting one side for discussion, we guide the client to validate the good intentions of both sides without encouraging or endorsing the very extreme behaviors on opposite limits of the spectrum. For example, it's essential to function, grow, and be responsible—but it's also essential to feel carefree, rested, and satisfied. We show managers and firefighters how they are linked, and we assure them that the client needs *both* teams for their complete well-being. As they begin to feel validated and safer, they will become more cooperative.

IS PSYCHOTHERAPY ENOUGH?

For clients who struggle with addictive processes that involve high-risk, self-harming behavior, psychotherapy isn't always enough. Some people need intense outpatient treatment or hospitalization. Peer support groups work wonders for many, but not all. Some will benefit from medication or the support of other professionals, such as a nutritionist or an acupuncturist. Some could use an adjunctive treatment, like couple therapy, art therapy, or a meditation group. Some won't be willing to use these kinds of options, and some won't have access to them. We can expect progress to go in fits (which we call recurrences) and starts (which is called progress). But whether an individual seeks help in a community mental health center, residential treatment, or private practice, psychotherapy is a central resource.

So let's drill down on this question: *What can we do in the therapy hour?* We can assert that the client's addictive process is fueled by the need to relieve emotional pain, we can offer clarity that normalizes their inner battles and helps to organize chaotic thinking, and we can show them how to get lasting relief by safely healing old wounds.

SECTION III

Assessment

Before we describe *how* an IFS therapist might assess an addictive process, we want to comment on a couple of concerns about the standard assessment approach for addictions. First, many addiction treatment programs, mental health clinics, and hospitals arrange their intake process around a traditional set of questions that assess the individual's use of drugs, alcohol, food, gambling, cybersex, and other potentially problematic preoccupations. These questionnaires have a pointed emphasis on addictive behaviors and often make no inquiry into the ways the client is functional and productive. As a result, they likely set the client up for internal backlash after the intake.

Second, clients who struggle with addictive processes are likely to go through many chapters of treatment, so by the time they get to your door, they may have been in treatment before, and they may have been told they couldn't be helped or that they didn't really want help. And if they reveal their addictive process right away, you may believe you should refer them to an addiction specialist. This is the norm. Treatment providers who are trained in traditional psychotherapy approaches typically try to avoid working with clients who engage in addictive behaviors, particularly those who use substances.

The prevailing view about substance use is that people who use substances need specialized help. As a result, even long-term clients who reveal an addictive process are often referred out (Interlandi, 2022). The therapists who refer out mean well and, on its face, their decision allows the client to get help from an expert who knows how to navigate addictive processes. If the client is in a life-threatening situation, stabilizing treatment is indeed the best course. But if the client has finally worked up the courage to confess a shameful secret and you send them off to start over with someone new, you have confirmed their deepest fear: *When I reveal myself, I'm rejected.* This amounts to telling a client that they must somehow "fix" the very problem they are seeking to address in therapy *before* they can receive your help.

This approach, in our view, impairs the effectiveness of clinical intervention from its first moments. For one thing, ambivalent clients may not follow through with referral suggestions, and even if they do follow through and manage to land a spot in an addiction treatment program (by no means a guarantee for people who don't have a lot of financial backing), the addiction specialists they see are likely to consider them uncooperative and lacking in willpower if they express a fear of sobriety or any reluctance to follow treatment recommendations. It's not unusual to hear treatment providers say that clients need to hit rock bottom before they will be serious about therapy. Likewise, it is often standard practice to give ambivalent clients additional hoops to jump through—for example, requiring that they complete intensive-outpatient treatment or attend a certain number of 12-step meetings—before they are allowed to have therapy. It is as if clients who use substances as part of their addictive process must *earn* the right to talk about their experience.

All this, in our view, indicates that generalist therapists have learned to fear—even dread—interactions with clients' firefighter parts, and they believe only specialists in addiction are equipped to handle treatment they view as a battle. The sequestering of substance use treatment and low expectations for success on the professional side, coupled with high drop-out and recurrence rates on the client side, all suggest that our prevailing treatment approaches aren't serving any of us very well. We believe that clients who aren't interested in total abstinence but are willing to talk about their substance use should be welcomed in therapy. We trust that their firefighter parts have reason to fear getting help, and we also know that many other parts of the client desperately want help.

If seeing clients with substance use worries you, try thinking of it this way. Most clients struggle with thought and mood issues that affect their ability to be present and function well. And those who don't use substances are often heavily engaged in some type of self-regulating, compulsive activity, such as chronic gaming, watching porn, or overexercising. Whether or not a client is, as the saying goes, "clean and sober," therapy can be very effective. We agree that clinicians need to be clear about the limitations of their role and maintain kind, firm boundaries, but this is true of interactions with any client who is blended with a firefighter part. Referring clients to a specialized treatment program is only imperative when their substance use is life-threatening, but this does not include the majority of clients. In IFS, we commit to collaborating with clients, reframing addictive processes, and articulating hope.

CREATING A CONTEXT FOR COLLABORATION AND HOPE

Hospitals, clinics, and addiction treatment programs have standard assessment forms that clients fill out in the context of a larger process called an intake evaluation. A staff member or trainee walks the client through the assessment questions to get as much factual information about them and their history as possible. The interviewer is a stranger and an evaluative authority figure who the client may never see again.

We have a bone to pick with this approach. A fact-finding interview with a narrow line of questioning (which coaxes tell-tale information about self-destructive behavior in excruciating detail) summons a fragile, shamed person to the punitive court of self-judgment. It's intrusive and it establishes a hierarchical relationship that can easily evoke fear and defensiveness. It also fails to explore the ways in which the client is productive and tells us little about how they are navigating inner conflict, which is a crucial feature of addictive processes. The standard assessment approach puts the interviewer in a one-up manager position with authority over the one-down, troubled client and is a disservice to both parties. In these ways, it is antithetical to the IFS approach.

In our first therapy session with a client, we are careful not to start by urging them to expose their most shame-inducing secrets. Just like the client and the interviewer in a standard assessment, the client and the therapist are initially strangers to each other. Therefore, in IFS therapy, our first aim is to create a safe, collaborative context. We view assessment as a process that occurs over time. Instead of launching into an investigation, we get curious, avoid assumptions, and ask a lot of open-ended questions—

and we continue in this vein in every session thereafter. We learn the client's history and assess their functioning over time. We understand that larger institutions create standard criteria for evaluation in order to maintain a certain level of care and to ensure that clients get what they need, so we don't mean to minimize the challenges of changing the standard approach. But we do have strong views about what works best for clients.

The importance of a first session is that it leads to a second session. We can't help people if they don't show up. In IFS, we take a nonjudgmental stance and offer compassion from the beginning, recognizing that the client's willingness to disclose their struggles is hard-won and courageous. As therapists, we aim to embody what we call the 5 P's: Our patience, perseverance, and perspective are reassuring and calming—while our presence and playfulness are engaging. We notice the client's parts as they operate in the three categories of manager, firefighter, and exile. We offer a reframe to their struggles by eliciting and validating the positive intentions of polarized protective teams. And, above all, we offer hope: *You can feel better, and I can be your guide.*

---

5 P's ROLE OF THE THERAPIST

- **Patience:** We know that building trust takes time.

- **Perseverance:** We offer hope and stay on message.

- **Perspective:** We look at how far a client has come, not how far they have to go.

- **Playfulness:** We use humor as appropriate to ease tension.

- **Presence:** We are fully engaged with the client.

Research shows that the quality of the therapeutic relationship is directly related to the outcome of treatment, and this is particularly important for clients who engage in addictive processes (Miller & Rollnick, 2013). When the therapeutic relationship is safe, the client can make solid inner connections. In IFS, the therapist's Self and the client's Self are two healers in collaboration, taking the bird's eye view of addiction treatment, looking at the whole system, and seeing the totality of the client's progress over time. We trust that the client's story will unfold and that they will reveal new information about their pattern of use as their protectors feel comfortable. When this happens, we take it as a very positive sign. We model the respectful, collaborative relationship style that we know warring parts can develop as exiles heal in relationship with the client's Self.

Try Banning a Soothing, Distracting Firefighter Part to See How It Feels[*]

The purpose of this exercise is to notice and identify which parts of you activate when you are permanently deprived of a favorite activity or behavior. This will help you understand the reluctance and fear many clients exhibit when they are told they must get sober or never engage in a particular activity ever again. Remember that all parts serve a purpose, and for clients with addictive processes, the prospect of banning a soothing or distracting firefighter can be frightening.

First, get comfortable. You can lie on the floor or sit up if you prefer. Begin by focusing on your breathing. If it feels comfortable, put one hand over your heart and the other on your belly. Take a few moments to breathe deeply into these two emotional centers. When you're ready, think of an activity you particularly enjoy. It might be something like watching funny movies, cooking, eating a favorite food, exercising, walking in the woods, or reading. Don't choose an activity or food item that is controversial for your system. Pick one that brings you genuine enjoyment without any conflict attached to it.

Now, watch yourself engaging in this activity. Notice your facial expressions and body language. When you're ready, connect to the part associated with this behavior. How much does it enjoy engaging in this behavior? How important is the behavior to the part? Perhaps it feels very important, somewhat important, or even unimportant.

Then ask the part if it is willing to play a game that may cause some distress but will teach you some important information. If it agrees, say that the game is beginning, and tell the part that it can never engage in this favorite behavior again. Not ever. If the part tries to negotiate for more time with this behavior, be very firm and insist that the behavior can never happen again. It is completely over.

Notice any reactions to this news in your body, including any thoughts as you say, "No, never again." If any parts protest to the ban, tell them they are bad if they can't agree to stop the behavior. You may notice some activation in your belly that feels

_____

[*] The concept for this exercise originated from IFS Senior Trainer Mary Kruger.

like worry, anxiety, or fear. You may notice a thought response along the lines of: *Hey! You can't do that.* Perhaps you notice disbelief. Maybe a part says, "Don't worry, I'll still find a way" or "You can't tell me what to do." Connect to the parts who react and ask how this change would affect them. You may want to ask what concerns they have about giving up this activity. Again, tell them if they can't stop, they are being bad.

Finally, reassure all your parts that this was just an experiment and that it is actually fine for them to continue doing what they enjoy. Notice what that statement feels like in your body, including any thoughts or comments that come up. Take a few minutes to write about your experience. How did this experiment in deprivation feel to your system? What was it like for your parts to be told what to do and to have no recourse? How did it feel to be judged when they objected? Finally, how might this experience inform or support you in connecting with a client who comes to you for help with an addictive process?

_____

_____

_____

_____

_____

_____

_____

_____

_____

_____

_____

_____

_____

_____

_____

Explore Your Reaction to the Words *Addict* and *Addiction*

This exercise is designed to mildly activate any parts of you that hold conscious or unconscious bias about the words *addict* or *addiction*. Since these terms are commonly used in the field of substance use treatment, this exercise is designed to help you explore any unseen reactivity that these words elicit. If you think it will be too activating for you, do not do this exercise alone. Invite a friend or colleague to do it with you and support each other.

Find a quiet place and make yourself comfortable, taking a few minutes to adjust your position until you feel physically at ease or at rest. If it feels okay, close your eyes, inviting even your eyes to rest and enjoy doing less. Then focus on your breathing, and try extending your inhalations and exhalations to the count of seven, eight, or nine. Notice your deeper breath as your body settles. Take time to enjoy this feeling of self-regulation.

When you are ready, focus internally on your thoughts and emotions. Take your time simply focusing on your inner experience. Now say the word *addict* to yourself a few times or repeat the word *addiction*. As you do this out loud or internally, notice your body, feelings, and thoughts. Notice any images that come to mind. Perhaps a real or an imagined "addict" came to your mind's eye. If so, how do you feel toward that person? What do you notice yourself thinking about that person? Do you have the urge to get away from that person or take care of them?

Maybe the word itself, without any images, activates some parts in your system. Do these parts feel sad, angry, fed up, frustrated, hopeless, or helpless? Notice all the parts who react to the words *addict* or *addiction*. Say hello to these parts, and if it feels right, be curious and ask them to share the origin of their reaction to those words. When you understand, let them know.

When your exchange feels complete, appreciate them for sharing with you. Then bring your attention back and take some time to draw or journal about your experience.

_____

_____

FROM STANDARD ASSESSMENT TO IFS ASSESSMENT

The majority of standard addiction questionnaires range from 6 to 25 questions in length and are focused solely on assessing the client's addiction symptoms. These forms ask clients to report on the frequency of their addictive behavior, increases in patterns of use, levels of preoccupation, mood changes, and any associated impact on their ability to complete daily tasks. They also ask about negative feedback from partners and family members. Some ask if there is any history of addiction, violence, abuse, or neglect in the client's family of origin. All this scrutiny at once, as we've suggested, is potentially shaming and overwhelming for new clients—not only for those who have been victimized at some point in their lives but also those who have been the perpetrator. There is a huge overlap between substance use and domestic violence, and while we don't minimize the impact of violent parts, it never pays to exile a part, even one who is guilty of a transgression (Schwartz, 2016).

In IFS, our very first intervention is an optimistic, nonjudgmental attitude. If we are patient and open-minded, compulsive firefighter parts will talk with us. We don't need to minimize the deleterious effects of their behavior or give these parts a pass in order to be interested in the benefits they pursue. And on this topic, firefighters have a lot to say. Clients need to understand how they have benefited from firefighter behaviors and how each behavior is a clue to an unmet need. In IFS, we call these clues *trailheads,* and we view them as an invitation that says, "Come this way!" As we go down that path in therapy with compassionate, mindful attention, the client hears from parts who kept them alive in tough times, and they start to build internal relationships that will heal their attachment wounds.

As we guide clients to befriend their parts and understand their motives, we find out who is ready to try something new—and who isn't. We expect ambivalence. If the client is in our office after years of trying to change, we know it hasn't worked out yet. But their willingness to try again indicates that some (or many!) of their parts are ready to try again. At the same time, we know they have other parts who feel differently. Some are afraid of feeling too much, some are afraid of people, and some enjoy using. Mixed feelings and multiple perspectives are normal, and together they call for inquiry. People who are caught in a cycle of physical cravings, emotional pain, and all-too-temporary relief desperately need to inquire inside, as this sustained, compassionate reflection can lead to healing.

Physician and author Gabor Maté suggests setting aside the question "Why this addiction?" to instead ask, "Why this pain?" Similarly, IFS therapists set aside the question "Why are you invested in self-destructive behavior?" to ask, "How are your parts trying to help you?" We abstain from the question "Why are you so checked out?" to ask, "What are you afraid would happen if you didn't use this substance (or engage in this activity) anymore?" We want to hear about the needs that lie underneath extreme behavior, and we get that information by including all of the client's parts. IFS offers a set of clear, kind interventions that avoid taking sides and start where the client is today.

Advice for Therapists Who Create Their Own Assessment

If you have the freedom to formulate your own initial evaluation, we recommend not using a lengthy initial assessment of the client's history of addictive processes and their attempts to be abstinent. Your goal for the first contact is to engage the client. Remember, you want people who seek help to be willing to come back and get help.

While assessing someone's addictive process, it's also important to recall that different clients will initially have different end goals. Clients who reveal their firefighter parts but don't talk about their managers will certainly be allergic to the notion of abstinence. You can locate this aversion by asking what they've been told about abstinence. Many will have heard that any other outcome is failure. This question will also let you clarify your approach. The IFS therapist aims to help clients be in relationship with their parts—not to control them.

If a client needs prompt intervention to stay alive, there isn't much room for negotiation. But even (or especially) then, it helps to assert that harsh managers and extreme firefighters all mean well, that exiles can be healed, and that the client is welcome to continue therapy after their inpatient stay. This kind of warm reassurance can go a long way toward winning cooperation.

Advice for Therapists Who Are Required to Take a Traditional Addiction History

If you work in an institution that uses an addiction history questionnaire, you can sidestep some of the problems mentioned earlier by joining with the client and giving yourself a bit of distance from the institution. For example, you might say something like "The clinic needs us to fill out this form. After that, we can talk about what you need and what you're looking for." After filling out the questionnaire, you can survey the client's parts, both the ones who help them function (often quite well) in various arenas and the ones who engage in addictive behaviors. As you go about this evaluation, you'll want to assess—just for yourself at this point—the role of the part who is taking the lead in this first interview. Is it a firefighter, a manager, or an exile?

HOW THE IFS THERAPIST STARTS THERAPY

- Welcome the client's full system of parts and talk with any blended parts by using implicit direct access.

- Ask why they seek help now, and listen for conflicting parts in their answer.

- Support their courage in reaching out.

- Dive into the language and perspective of the model by reflecting back with parts language (e.g., some parts want to control the behavior of other parts, some parts worry about their functioning, some parts like to use).

- Explain that you see the client's parts as an inner community (or family) that's engaged in a repetitive battle over how to stay safe.

- When a client presents with urgency and seems unambiguous about addressing their addictive behaviors, assume you are only hearing one side in an ongoing argument.

- Although it may feel counterintuitive, engage with parts who want to keep using. They are nervous and suspicious about seeking help. They need to know that you care about their perspective.

- Invite skeptical parts on both sides of this polarity: the ones who are reluctant to trust and the ones who are tired of the chaos, instability, and health concerns.

- Assume that parts are burdened by doubts and may be terrified about trying once again to get help.

WHEN A FIREFIGHTER PRESENTS FIRST

Firefighters are good at avoiding direct answers and may leave you with the distinct impression that the client is minimizing their level of use or other addictive behavior. A firefighter might, for example, rationalize the client's situation as a single, current crisis that will never happen again. It might also insist that the overblown concerns of other people are the real problem, outright deny having a problem, or complain about whoever mandated the client to get help. Whatever their strategy, this no-big-deal attitude puts the therapist in a bind. Do you take a firmer stance and insist on answers that sound more honest? Or accept the futility of a power struggle and go with vague half-answers of doubtful truthfulness?

If you assume a more confrontational stance with firefighters, you automatically form an alliance against them—and *with* the client's manager parts. But if you don't challenge them at all, you're excluding managers from the conversation. Neither option is good. Just as excluded managers will eventually step in with a vengeance, firefighters will take over at some point if they are dismissed. So what do you do?

Luckily, you don't have to join with managers or outfox firefighters. It's easier and more effective to simply ask the client if they ever hear from the other side.

For example, Roger, a thirty-eight-year-old, Irish American, heterosexual, married, cisgender man, was employed in construction management. He was depressed, and his use of alcohol and cannabis had recently increased dramatically. His wife insisted that he go to therapy. This was his third session.

WORKING WITH A FIREFIGHTER

Therapist: How are you, Roger?

Roger's Firefighter: Not great really. My wife is not talking to me. We got into it last night because I was hanging out in the garage and she is *so* sick of it.

Therapist: Sounds stressful. When you say, "hanging in the garage," do you mean you were drinking?

Roger's Firefighter: Yeah, I was out there till midnight or something.

Therapist: Uh-huh. So, you headed out there after work or…?

Roger's Firefighter: Well, I went into the house when I got home. But then, yeah, I had a case in my truck and, ya know, some weed, and I went out to the garage. I've got a TV out there and everything.

Therapist: Right. So by the time you went back into the house, everyone was asleep and you were pretty loaded.

Roger's Firefighter: Yeah. I slept on the couch and when I got up for work, my wife just started ragging on me. She thinks I never see the kids and she has to do everything. She says I'm embarrassing her.

Therapist: When you're doing your thing and not with her and the kids, she is angry and maybe disappointed, too.

Roger's Firefighter: I really don't need to hear that shit. I had a huge thing going on at work and I don't need to get screamed at before I'm half-awake in the morning.

Therapist: I hear you. It's stressful to be yelled at. And you were probably not feeling that great.

Roger's Firefighter: No. I wasn't! She's not considerate. She could lay off for once!

Therapist: Right. I do get that. It's like she's angry with you so often. Can I ask one question? (*Roger nods.*) When your wife is accusing you of not being around, of getting loaded and not being with the kids, have you ever said the same thing to yourself? Maybe when you first wake up in the morning?

> This is an unblending question. The therapist has been speaking directly with the firefighter—without directly naming the part and by instead using the pronoun *you*, which means this is *implicit direct access*. The therapist now asks the client to notice other parts.

Roger's Firefighter: Say what to myself? I don't have time to say shit before she starts in on me.

Therapist: Right, this morning you woke up to an angry wife. But my question is more general. If not this morning, have you ever had a similar thought? Like you were shaving and you looked in the mirror and thought, *Okay, maybe I am hitting it too hard*. Or you had a kind of a guilty feeling about the kids, like that you haven't been around for them much. Is that possible? Have you ever had your *own* worries about all this?

> The therapist persists.

Roger's Firefighter: Well with her going on and on like I'm doing this every day, which I do not—

Therapist: (*Therapist interrupts.*) Yes, I get it. You feel like your wife can't see any of the good things about you anymore. But aside from her, aside from her anger with you, I'm wondering if *you* have ever said something similar to yourself, like *I need to cut back* or *That headache is just too big when I get up in the morning*.

> The therapist interrupts the firefighter, parenthetically acknowledges its point, and persists.

Roger: Ever? You mean have I ever felt shitty about drinking and getting high and all that?

> Roger's Self starts to come online as he gets a little space from the firefighter, enough to acknowledge that he has manager parts.

Therapist: Right, have you ever worried a little bit about yourself?

Roger: Well, yeah. I mean it's not the greatest to spend the night in the fucking garage getting fucked up. I mean, yeah, it's not like I want to be doing this for the rest of my life. But she acts like that's all I do, like I live out there. And last weekend I went to see her sister with her and the kids—

> The firefighter jumps in again.

Therapist: (*Therapist interrupts.*) I know. I do know that your wife has her own perspective and it doesn't match yours. But am I hearing it correctly that, aside from her view, you have your own feeling, your own sense of things, which, at times, says you are using a little more than is healthy for you?

> The therapist again interrupts the firefighter, parenthetically acknowledges its point, and persists.

Roger: Sure, there have been days I feel bad about it.

> Roger acknowledges his polarity.

Therapist: Okay. So what I hear is that you have a part, or maybe a few parts, who like to get high and just want to be left alone to do their thing, right? (*Roger nods.*) And you have a whole other set of parts who can be critical of that, who say that those drinking parts go too far, that using is causing problems.

> The therapist lays out the polarity between Roger's parts.

Roger: Okay. I guess that's true.

Therapist: It's not an easy way to live, is it? Going back and forth between using and then getting mad at yourself and trying not to use. And then feeling like you have to use again, and so on.

> The therapist paints the big picture.

Roger: Yeah, that's my life.

> Roger is more unblended now and better able to take the bird's eye view.

Therapist: We can do something about that. If you're up for it, we can try something right now. (*Roger nods.*) Okay, let's set it up. Invite all these parts to come sit with you at a big table. You sit at the head of the table and put the substance-using parts who want time to chill and like getting loaded on one side. Then put the other parts—the ones who aren't happy about getting high—on the other side.

> When protectors are polarized, a conference with both sides helps everyone to unblend. It's like a poker game where everyone keeps their hands on the table.

Roger: Okay. Now what?

Therapist: If you had a work meeting, and the people on one side of the table wanted to move forward with a project but the people on the other side didn't, you'd listen to both sides, right? (*Roger nods.*) So let each side know that you're going to listen to them all. They all have important views. Ask if they're willing to take a break from fighting with each other and shift over to talking with you, just for now.

Roger: Okay. But it's not like they trust me.

Therapist: Of course not. Tell them you see their distrust, and, going forward, you're going to earn their trust because they're all important to you.

Roger: Well... (*He chuckles.*) here's one thing they can *all* agree on: We've got a way to go here!

Therapist: Very true. We do. But you're on your way now. This is new. Are you willing to stay with them so they feel less alone?

Roger: Okay, okay. Yeah, they do feel alone. They like me being here.

If the client has been mandated to treatment, which happens often to people who engage in costly compulsive behaviors, questions like "What brings you to therapy?" may elicit complaints and defensiveness from a blended firefighter part, as we saw with Roger, or even paranoia about the therapist's motives rather than hope and a willingness to engage. Roger began this session by focusing on his wife's anger rather than his behavior and its impact on her and their kids. His angry, defensive, substance-using parts spoke as if her anger was unjustified. They expressed no empathy and had no interest in understanding how his absences and drinking affected the family. Nor were they inclined to see that using was a problem for him.

The therapist could have justifiably supported his wife's point of view, but that would mean polarizing with firefighters who weren't yet feeling comfortable enough to be honest or ask for help. Alternatively, the therapist could have challenged Roger when he said his wife's wrath was out of line, hoping he would see reason and admit that his drinking was causing problems. But with both of those options, the therapist would have been challenging Roger's firefighter stance.

This IFS therapist had a different aim, which was to help Roger discover his other team: the managers who felt responsible for and concerned about his substance use and who were worried about his family. In his initial firefighter narrative, Roger complained about other people, and his managers weren't audible. But the therapist knew they existed and were trying to control his drinking. The therapist knew that these two protector teams were fighting with each other inside. To help Roger stop projecting this internal conflict into his relationships with his wife and kids (or his relationship with the therapist), the therapist stayed curious and asked if Roger was sometimes angry with himself. When he finally admitted to some self-criticism, the therapist was able to help him meet his polarized teams. As Roger sat at the head of the table as a third party who could welcome the positive intentions of both sides, he was able to collaborate with the therapist and begin to build Self-to-part relationships with his managers and firefighters.

WHEN A MANAGER PRESENTS FIRST

The previous interaction with Roger illustrates how we dig around for evidence of concern when we talk with blended firefighter parts, but if we're talking with a manager, we take another tack, which is to validate their concerns and check for exhaustion and a willingness to try something new. Consider the case of Helen, a forty-eight-year-old, Mexican American, single, cisgender woman, who had been bulimic and in therapy for most of her teenage years. She was no longer bingeing and purging, but she was intensely worried about smoking the occasional cigarette and what she called "unhealthy eating" at night. This eating was interfering with her sleep and her ability to function during the day. She also reported, by way of background information, that she was spending most weekends with old friends drinking, taking pills, and using cannabis.

Many clients engage in more than one firefighter activity. Disordered eating and substance use are a common combination. Since it sounded like Helen's eating issue was relatively mild, a part of the therapist wanted to prioritize Helen's chronic, heavy weekend substance use. However, the therapist set that sense of imperative aside (without ignoring it) in order to meet Helen in the here and now, help her understand her system, and get some clarity and immediate relief.

WORKING WITH A MANAGER

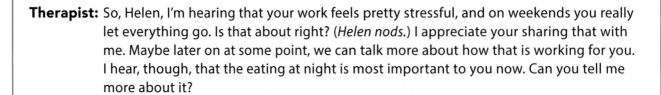

Therapist: So, Helen, I'm hearing that your work feels pretty stressful, and on weekends you really let everything go. Is that about right? (*Helen nods.*) I appreciate your sharing that with me. Maybe later on at some point, we can talk more about how that is working for you. I hear, though, that the eating at night is most important to you now. Can you tell me more about it?

Helen's Manager: Yeah, the weekends are *fine*—I need my weekends!

Therapist: I hear you. You need your weekends.

> Helen is blended with her substance-using firefighter parts. The therapist doesn't challenge them but takes note internally that Helen needs to use.

Helen's Manager: But I have to get over this eating thing! I was so tired at work today because last night I got up at 2 a.m. to eat cereal, which is ridiculous. So then I smoked a few cigarettes, which I have to stop because it's disgusting. And it took me till 4 a.m. to get back to sleep. This has been going on for months. I can't take it anymore! And it's going to happen again tonight.

Therapist: I hear you're worried and stressed. This feels odd and it affects you at work the next day. But you can't get a handle on it.

> The therapist is speaking directly to Helen's worried, frustrated managers, which reflects direct access. Helping them feel understood will help them unblend.

Helen's Manager: It's screwing me up, that's for sure! I'm sick of it. It's so disgusting. I try to make myself go back to sleep, but I can't. Nothing works. I need to get over this. It shouldn't be this hard!

Therapist: Let me reflect back what I'm hearing and the parts I'm noticing. (*Helen nods.*) I'm hearing a team of parts—we'll call them your manager team—who are very concerned about the nightly eating. One critical part closely watches all that eating and hates it. A judging part is also disgusted by the eating and the smoking. Then I notice a very urgent, maybe even desperate controlling part that says this has to stop. And I think I hear even another harsh and perfectionistic part who says it should not be so hard to stop. These parts are driven to change the parts who are eating and smoking in the night; we'll call them your soother team.

Helen's Manager: Yeah, they need to change all right.

> Helen is blended with the manager team.

Therapist: But the eating and smoking parts don't seem to be listening, is that right? The soother team is back at it every night, no matter how much the critical, judging, and perfectionistic parts yell at them. And maybe there's one more little part in the background who gets scared and feels hopeless about getting it right? (*Helen nods and shrugs, as this is all very familiar.*) Let's invite them all to come sit with you at a big conference table. You sit at the head, and they can sit opposite each other. Do you see them? And do they see you? (*Helen nods.*) If the scared, hopeless one wants to be there, put it across from you at the foot of the table for now. Which team needs your attention first, Helen?

Helen's Manager: I need to work on the eating! So, the cereal-eating part.

Therapist: Okay great. Let's connect with that part. Can you see yourself eating cereal at night?

Helen's Manager: I see myself sitting on the couch with a big bowl of cereal.

Therapist: Okay, so just sit back and observe her. What is her expression? What is her body language? How do you feel toward her, as you watch?

Helen's Manager: She's pathetic. She just sits there shoveling it in. It's depressing to look at her.

> The therapist notices their own parts cringing in response to this harshness.

Therapist: Hmm, okay, so you have a part who feels judgmental toward the cereal-loving one. It's disgusted and critical.

Helen's Manager: Yes, because the eating is disgusting.

Therapist: I get it. The cereal-eater is, like, in a trance? (*She nods.*) And you can hear how hard the critic comes down on her?

Helen's Manager: Well, eating in the night is a terrible habit! And then because I can't stop and I'm afraid I'll gain weight, I smoke. But I hate smoking! And every night when I go to bed, I say *Maybe I won't get up and do it tonight*. But I do and I don't know why. Oh, I hate myself!

Therapist: Your managers are afraid for you because you're not in control in the middle of the night. And the smoking part tries to help with the risk of weight gain. Let's pause for a minute and appreciate them. Do they notice you?

Helen: Okay yeah, I guess they know I'm trying to listen. But they hate me.

Therapist: The critic does really hate some of your other parts, but it doesn't hate *you* because it doesn't know you yet. Let it know that you're listening, and you know it hates the parts who eat and smoke in the night. But you are not them. You are the one who listens to everyone. The critic is talking to you now.

Helen: It did think I was the cereal-eating part. Hmm.

Therapist: The cereal-eating part certainly does exist. Ask the critic why it needs to hate the cereal-eating part. How is it trying to help you?

Helen: It hates her because she is so totally into her food and it thinks she'll get worse. Like she'll start throwing up again and eating more.

Therapist: That makes sense. And that would be really bad. Has the critic seen the cereal-eating part be much worse than it is now?

> The therapist is helping Helen tune in to the critic's intention, which is to prevent a recurrence of firefighter behavior and appreciate that the critic has seen Helen suffer from bulimia during her teenage years, so its fear is legitimate.

Helen: Well yeah, it's seen me worse, of course. I mean, I used to throw up all time. My eating was crazy. My life was totally messed up.

Therapist: That was a super tough time. Let the critic know you get it. It was a long time ago, but the critic has a point! The bingeing and purging parts were out of control and ran your life back then. You understand that, right, Helen?

Helen: Yeah, I know how bad that was. I get why it's trying to stop the cereal-eating part now.

Therapist: There is a different option now, though. If you connected with the cereal-eater and the smoker and helped them, would the critic, judge, and perfectionist be willing to let go a little bit?

Helen: They're not so sure about that!

Therapist: There's no rush. But they should know that the eating and smoking parts mean well. There's more to them than meets the eye. If we could connect with them and help them use their energy in a different way, would that be good?

Helen: Well, if we could, it would be good. But the critic isn't convinced. It doesn't think I have any influence.

Therapist: Well, you would have to demonstrate that, wouldn't you? Would they step back and let you connect with the eating and smoking parts, just for a few minutes, here in our session, to show what you can do?

Helen: Okay, okay. They'll let me try. They're so tired of all this.

Therapist: They're tired. But with you here, they're not alone anymore. (*Helen relaxes visibly.*)

In IFS, we aim for therapy to be an accepting, safe container for shaming managers, as well as shameless firefighters and exiles who feel shameful. Manager fears are completely reasonable based on what they know from the past. We assure them that the client's Self can help the firefighter team (which also has good intentions) to behave more responsibly. Helen came to this session feeling anxious about her lack of sleep and totally blended with critics who were attacking her cereal-eating and smoking parts. Although she spoke of a team of weekend warriors who were using heavily, her managers were most afraid of the unwelcome night visitors and their effect on her work performance, and we want to respect the client's priorities. As Helen experienced relief from her initial concerns, she was able to focus more directly on painful early childhood issues, eventually addressing her weekend activities as well.

WHEN AN EXILE PRESENTS FIRST

Finally, there are times when a client presents in therapy while blended with an exiled part. You can tell that the client is blended with an exile (or is in imminent threat of being blended with an exile) if they present in a state of collapse or near collapse. They may appear crumpled, cringing, tearful, overwhelmed, or dissociated (a firefighter responding to the blended exile). If the therapist's protectors are inclined to over-function or distance from the client in these situations, the therapist will need to help their own protective parts step back first. Only then can the therapist help the client's protectors unblend so the client's Self can become available, welcoming the exile with plenty of compassion for its panicked state. To facilitate this Self-to-part connection, the therapist reflects back what the client is communicating. The therapist may also want to pause the client and initiate a moment of unblending by inviting the client to take a breath and appreciate how much their parts have been holding all week. This step recruits the observational perspective of the Self, if briefly.

For example, Luna, a twenty-seven-year-old Italian American, cisgender, single, heterosexual woman, first came to therapy for generalized anxiety, depression, and posttraumatic stress disorder. She arrived at her twentieth session very anxious and at one point folded over in her chair, barely able to talk as she sobbed.

WORKING WITH AN EXILE

Therapist: I'm going to talk with this part directly, Luna. I want to speak with the part who is upset. Are you there?

Luna's Exile: (*After a long pause, she speaks in a small voice.*) Yes.

Therapist: You're welcome here. I want you to know that. Do you protect any other part? (*Luna shakes her head no.*) Would you like help? (*She nods.*) Good. Because we want to help you. I'm going to explain what you can do to make sure that happens. Okay? (*Luna nods.*) While there are parts who keep you hidden, Luna also has a Self—who is not a part—who can help you. Luna's Self can talk with the ones who keep you hidden. With their permission, she can help you. Meanwhile, we can put you in a safe place. Would that be good?

> We assert the crucial difference between the client's Self and their parts while leaving the door open for the client to understand the Self in their own way.

Luna's Exile: (*She continues in the small voice.*) Yes.

> Seeing the benefit of cooperating, the exile agrees to unblend.

Therapist: Great. Where would you like to be?

Luna's Exile: The waterfall.

Therapist: Good. Be at the waterfall. Do you need anything there?

Luna's Exile: My dog.

Therapist: For sure. Bring your dog. Now I'm going to talk with Luna. Are you there, Luna?

Luna: Yes.

Therapist: How are other parts responding?

Luna: They like it.

Therapist: Any concerns?

Luna: What if the upset part gets overwhelmed again?

Therapist: We'll help her stay at the waterfall until you have permission to help her.

Luna: Okay.

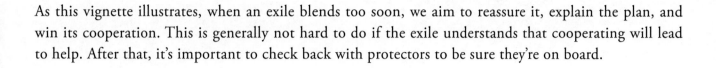

As this vignette illustrates, when an exile blends too soon, we aim to reassure it, explain the plan, and win its cooperation. This is generally not hard to do if the exile understands that cooperating will lead to help. After that, it's important to check back with protectors to be sure they're on board.

Treatment

THE THERAPIST ROLE: CONNECTION AND COLLABORATION

Our radical assumption in IFS is that everybody has an undamaged, strong, clear, calm essence and the capacity to function with agency. As a result, we have neither the right nor the authority to take any protection away from the client, including their methods of soothing and distracting. In IFS, we don't try to control clients and we don't judge them; we help them connect with their controlling and judgmental managers. We also don't argue with firefighters who are distracting from sadness and fear because doing so would amount to more distraction from the main issue, which is exiled pain.

By the same token, it is not our responsibility to determine the outcome of treatment. We assume clients have lost their access to Self-leadership and self-trust, but we also believe they still have the capacity for self-compassion and self-governance. We help them locate and build on it. To that end, our first and ongoing aim is to create order out of chaos. We welcome the client as they appear now (which is generally stressed out and overwhelmed by internal conflict), and as a way of building Self-to-part connections, we help them identify their parts, understand the roles of these parts, and see how they group together into teams. As the Self takes the lead, clients learn the intentions behind parts' behaviors and become willing to try alternative actions in the future. Like most therapy, this takes time.

The deeper the client's pain and disorganization, the longer and more intense the therapy—and the more pressure on the therapist's system. Addictive processes are uniquely stressful for the manager parts of therapists, who are prone to judging, caretaking, and panicking. The client's anxiety, turmoil, and risk-taking exert a centrifugal draw on the resources of everyone in their vicinity, especially therapists who have responsible managers. For these parts, it can take more energy to resist a bid for help than it takes to dive in with directives. But giving in to that urge will prove highly ineffective. Short of an acute crisis in which intervention is necessary, taking the bulk of decision-making out of the client's hands on a regular basis (which happens in many treatment centers) is bound to be counterproductive. We can forestall our caretaking, critical, and controlling parts from blending and siding with the client's managers by listening to our own protectors and helping our exiles as needed, with supervision if necessary (Redfern, 2022).

When we feel helpless and dismayed with our clients, we may become blended with our firefighter parts, who may want to escape the client's distress, punish their lies, or steer clear of their anger. Although it is only natural for our firefighters to respond this way when a client is damaging themself and hurting others, we still must prevent them from overtaking therapy. With this aim, we can quickly check inside, validate our reactive parts, normalize their feelings, and ask them to trust us. To the client, we may speak out loud about our need to press pause and collect our thoughts. If that's not possible, we can be transparent, letting the client know that one of our parts is reacting to one of their parts and naming our part.

Sometimes our exiles will escalate. We see them in panic, fearing incompetence, and full of shame. Although we may choose to speak for certain exiles when we are in session with a client—for example, naming them in the course of apologizing for a judgmental protector—we generally help our vulnerable parts outside of session. When we routinely make time for them, they are more willing to stay separate and wait for a bit when they need help.

That said, working closely with a system that is distressed and unbalanced can activate exiles and protectors in even the most level-headed clinician. When our protectors feel the need to activate, we go to our vulnerable parts. How have they been affected? What do they need to feel reassured right now? Whether or not we can ever unburden all of our exiles, we need to have the experience of feeling open-hearted compassion, negotiating with our protectors, witnessing our exiles, being with them as they unburden, and feeling their relief. This is how we gain the courage to befriend the firefighters of our clients and listen to their good intentions.

Any kind of parts takeover in the therapist that is not acknowledged, even if it's brief, will have a negative effect. Many clients have vigilant parts detectors and can easily perceive the therapist's parts. We become accountable by acknowledging our role in any relationship rupture, welcoming the client's feedback, and inviting them to tell us how it felt to be on receiving end of our behavior. By speaking for our parts and promising to care for them, we make a repair and preserve the safety of the therapeutic relationship.

We also model practicing what we preach. The client's protectors need to know that the therapist is on their side. Apologies can be a powerful intervention in this regard. There is no shame in us or our clients having protectors and exiles. As the Buddhist teacher Pema Chödrön (2007) wrote, "Compassion is not a relationship between the healer and the wounded. It's a relationship between equals. Only when we know our own darkness well can we be present with the darkness of others. Compassion becomes real when we recognize our shared humanity" (p. 50).

Common Therapist Managers

- **Controlling:** *You have to get rid of it!* (food, drugs, phone numbers, and so on)

- **Caretaking:** *I can call that agency for you.*

- **Judging:** *You should know better than that by now.*

- **Critical:** *Wow. That was a big mistake! You really blew it this time.*

- **Overly responsible:** *It's my fault this client isn't getting better. I should do more.*

- **Perfectionistic:** *That was okay, but this would have been better.*

Common Therapist Firefighters

- **Angry:** *This client doesn't even listen to me! They waste my time.*

- **Distracting:** *Let's just focus on your work situation today.*

- **Colluding:** *Yeah, it's not really that big a deal.*

- **Escapist:** *I'm sorry, but I have to cancel our appointment.*

- **Soothing:** *Tonight, I deserve _____* (to have a few drinks, get high, eat ice cream, watch TV, zone out on social media, and so on).

- **Dissociating:** *Can you repeat that?*

Common Therapist Exiles

- **Hopeless:** *This client is never going to change.*

- **Ashamed:** *I'm not good enough. I never get it right!*

- **Guilty:** *I am a terrible person. I'm not empathic enough.*

- **Overidentified:** *You're just like me.*

- **Overwhelmed:** *I don't know where to start.*

- **Sad:** *This reminds me of my childhood—it's too sad!*

Get to Know Three Sets of Parts

Therapists who are learning the IFS approach to addictive processes will encounter three sets of parts who have different interests and needs. In this exercise, we invite you to notice and reach out to each set of parts. You can do all three sections at once, but if that feels challenging, feel free to go more slowly and do each section at a different time. Read through to the end of this exercise before making a decision on how to proceed. If you think you would benefit from having someone to talk with, ask a colleague to do the exercise with you or to be available for a check-in once you've finished.

Here are the three sets of parts:

- Therapist parts who aim to learn new interventions and get new ideas for reaching your clients.

- Parts who focus on your family members or other loved ones who suffer from various addictive processes.

- Parts who focus internally, on your own addictive processes, whether in the past or currently. (If you can't think of a personal struggle that rises to the level of an addictive process, we invite you to think of any activity that causes some measure of internal conflict. For example, perhaps one part likes a certain activity but another part wants you to stop.)

Get ready to inquire into these three sets of parts. First, take time to find privacy, get into a comfortable seated position, and relax. If it's okay with you, close your eyes and take a few deep breaths. Breathe fully and deeply, stretching your inhalation all the way down your back and feeling the chair or floor that supports you. Then breathe out slowly. Repeat a few times.

Next, welcome your therapist parts—the ones who want new ideas for your clients. What do they want to learn about the addictive process? What are their strengths? What are their challenges? Are they preoccupied with any particular clients today? Do they hold any clients with addictive processes, even from the past, in your heart? Do they react to or find it hard to connect with any particular clients? Listen to these parts. When you're ready, write down their answers. How do you feel toward them now? Tell them you've been listening. Thank them for whatever they shared. Let them know they can stay in relationship with you.

_____

_____

_____

_____

_____

_____

_____

Now, turn to any parts who focus on family members or loved ones who have struggled with addictive processes in the past or who struggle now. Notice the images or memories they hold. If you'd like, write down the name of each family member or loved one. What do your parts want you to know about this person? How have they been affected by this person? Has your connection with this person changed at all (that is, gotten better or worse)? If so, what happened?

Take time to record what your parts are holding for each of the people mentioned. How are these parts doing now? Listen carefully. Do they notice you? What do they want you to learn from this manual? Thank them for whatever they shared. Let them know they can stay in relationship with you.

_____

_____

_____

_____

_____

_____

_____

Finally, when you are ready, invite any parts who promote some type of addictive process to serve you. What do you notice about them? How do you feel toward them? Do you notice any other parts reacting toward them? If so, ask the reactive ones to step back and trust you. How have they tried to help? What do the addictive parts need from you today? What do they want you to understand or learn from this manual? Take time to record their answers and thank them for whatever they shared. Let them know they can stay in relationship with you.

_____

_____

_____

_____

_____

_____

_____

_____

OUR AGENDA

In IFS, we don't come at protectors in an addictive system with our own change agenda. This stance may feel counterintuitive or even downright unethical for a couple of reasons. First, people whose addictive parts cause dysfunction for themselves are bound to annoy and worry both themselves and others. Second, therapists are trained (and thereafter continually urged) to pursue change in their clients. But with extreme protectors, it's most effective to think systemically, be optimistic, and have no agenda other than getting them connected to the Self and letting them explain their positive intentions. For this to happen, our own managers have to relax. We must be able help our clients be curious and compassionate by being curious and compassionate ourselves. This is what we call being Self-led.

What we know can help us be and remain Self-led throughout therapy. We know that exiled emotions and memories are connected to the client's addictive process. And once we get to know a client, we understand why their protectors deploy when they do, even if the client doesn't recognize the association at first. We also know that inner critics work hard in an addictive system, so we get curious about parts who are critical of other parts or who blame other people. To help clients make this connection, we invite them to slow down, turn their attention inside, notice what happened in the days or hours before they gave into an addictive urge, and notice what they feel right now. We know their needy parts feel desperate and abandoned. And we know that internal matters must improve before the client will try any new behaviors. Therefore, we do therapy with a system, not a symptom.

THE ADDICTION POLARITY

As you treat clients who are engaged in addictive processes, keep the following information front and center in your mind. Polarized protector teams are the norm in addictive processes—and these teams have very different perspectives. For managers, engaging in the compulsive behavior is like volunteering to drown. For firefighters, abstinence is like throwing your life jacket away as the waters are rising. As a result, it's good to consider whom you're talking with. If you're only hearing from one side, you can be assured that the other side exists and will take the floor at some point. To avoid reinforcing polarized conflicts, it's best to just assume that the client has long been bombarded with differing views about using, stopping using, and even showing up for an assessment interview or first session—and avoid taking a side.

If your head is spinning because the client is being obliviously contradictory—for example, saying, "I have to stop drinking!" and "Why is everyone so uptight about what I do after work?"—that means you're listening to an argument between the two teams in real time. In this case, your best option is to call the game: "I hear a part who wants to stop drinking... Now I hear a part who doesn't want to stop drinking." Combine your nonjudgmental interest with a light, polite tone that will signal to firefighters—the ones who are hardest to engage—that you might confound their negative expectations.

If the client starts therapy by complaining about having to be in therapy, someone in their life probably pushed them to get treatment and you're listening to a firefighter complain (as we illustrated in the example of Roger, whose wife pressed him to seek therapy). In this case, mirror back, validate the part's feelings about other people weighing in on their habit, and then guide the client to notice their manager team by soliciting contrary views: "Other people are concerned about you using. Do you ever say something similar to yourself? Like *I need to cut back. That headache is just too big when I get up in the morning. I'm tired of feeling sick every day* or *I'm worried that things are getting worse.*" As illustrated with Roger, you may need to repeat this question a few times before the client admits to having a managerial perspective on using. But once they do, you can state the polarity in plain language and guide them to ask both teams to the table to talk with their Self.

If, on the other hand, the client is worried about their level of use (or a particular consequence of using) and comes to therapy of their own incentive, you're talking with a manager and you can use the standard IFS approach: "You've come to therapy because you want to cut back on drinking, but you feel ambivalent. So one part of you wants to cut back, but another part wants a drink at the end of the day. Is that right? Let's hear from both of those parts. Does anyone object?" From this point, you can explore the polarity and help polarized protectors unblend simultaneously using the following techniques.

IDENTIFYING AN ADDICTIVE POLARITY

Here is summary of steps to take to unpack the addictive polarity:

- Start by inviting the client to discuss what they wish were different. Are they looking for a behavioral shift, a modification, or a new vision?

- Listen closely to the client's description of themselves and other people. If they are blended with a manager, they will sound critical and anxious and push for change. If they are blended with a firefighter, they will defend their substance use or compulsive behavior and dismiss the risks. If they are blended with an exile, they will sound hopeless, lost, and ashamed.

- Notice if any of your parts respond to this narrative with fear, judgment, or the urge to caretake, and ask these parts to unblend.

- Explain to the client that each of their parts has a role that fits into one of three categories, and ask permission to reflect what you are hearing back in parts language so you can illustrate these roles.

- Ask the client to visualize and identify each part. Make a list of the parts who have showed up, and ask the client to place them on two teams and visualize them in separate spaces.

- Acknowledge that both sides are entrenched and feel trapped, that some of their behaviors are risky, and that consequences are accruing.

- Identify the positive intentions of each side, and point out that both teams are trying to help despite the fact that they view each other as enemies. They are both trying to keep the system in balance. Normalize their polarity.

- Assert that each team is more complex than it looks. Invite them to see each other in a new way.

- Check in to see how this new perspective is landing with the client.

- Invite the two teams to connect with the Self, who can help everyone by taking care of exiled parts.

- Offer hope: *There is never an excuse, but there are always reasons, and we can address those reasons.*

Triangle Mapping for a Polarized System

Once you identify a client's addictive polarity, map it onto a triangle, which will show the client how their exiles and protectors interact. To begin, invite the client to draw an inverted triangle. Label managers at the top left point and firefighters at the top right point. Place the exile (or exiles) at the bottom point.

Then invite the client to turn their attention inside and notice their managers. List these parts at the manager point of the triangle. Next, have them once again turn their attention inside and notice their firefighters. List these parts at the firefighter point of the triangle. Finally, invite them to notice any exiles that come up during the exercise and to list these parts at the bottom of the triangle. (Instead of writing down their parts, the client may prefer to draw their parts or choose figures to represent their parts using sand tray toys, IFS-inspired cards, magazine cutouts, and so on.)

Once the client finishes listing all of their parts, ask them to jot down the intentions and fears of both protective teams and of the exile. The client may wish to draw solid lines between parts who are particularly allied and broken lines to show which parts are most in conflict. When the triangle drawing is complete, here are some questions you may want to ask:

- What do you observe now?

- How do you feel now?

- Which part-to-part relationships stand out?

- Which parts are most polarized?

- How do you feel toward your exile(s)?

- Have you met all of these parts before?

- Which part (or polarity) wants your attention first?

- What does this part (choose one specific part to focus on) want from you?

When this process is complete, thank the parts who showed up and save the triangle for future sessions. If the client wants, they can take it home and keep adding parts or details about the motives of the parts they know to date.

Strategies for Helping Polarized Parts
Unblend at the Same Time

When protectors can't trust each other because they are extremely at odds, we ask them to unblend at the same time. The techniques described here—the conference table, the two-hand scale, connecting in the body—all facilitate simultaneous unblending.

1. The Conference Table

The conference table is a user-friendly exercise in which the client's Self welcomes their risk-taking firefighter team, their controlling manager team, and their exiles to sit together at a table. This can become a recurring intervention that the client can evoke at home as well.

First, ask the client to sit at the head of a big conference table. Next, invite the protective teams to sit on opposite sides of the table, while exiles take a seat across from the client's Self, at the foot of the table. Once everyone is arranged, be sure that the client's Self is present at the head of the table. If not, the client can ask the part who is sitting in for them to join its team and to let the Self sit down.

Next, guide the client to validate both the firefighter and manager teams for their positive intentions, and assert that each of them is needed. They may want to get rid of each other, but the Self intends to keep everyone on board. Invite them to shift their gaze away from the others, look to the Self, and consider the possibility that they no longer have to challenge or fix each other because the Self will help the exiles they protect and set them free.

Then ask who needs attention first. When a target part (or team) volunteers, ask the client how they feel toward this part (or team). If they say something negative, help the reactive part unblend. You might need to facilitate some shuttle diplomacy to illustrate that the Self can handle both teams. Then listen to the target part (or team), validate its good intentions, explore the pros and cons of what it does, and ask if it is ready to try something new. Then do the same with the other side.

Finally, ask if it would be good for everyone if the Self could help the exiles that these two teams protect. When they agree, ask the client what they notice in their body now. If protectors are unblending, they will name a sense of space or calm or something along those lines. If exiles activate, invite them to sit with the Self. Reassure everyone that the Self is committed to the whole system and that no one is alone.[*]

2. The Two-Hand Scale

The two-hand scale is another way of helping polarized protectors unblend at simultaneously. To practice this exercise, invite the client to hold their hands palm up. Then instruct the client to close their eyes as you say, "Don't think. Put one part in one hand and the other part in the other hand. Which hand weighs more?" Then ask each hand, "What is your message?" End by asking the client, "How do you feel now toward these polarized teams now?"

3. Connect in the Body

Connecting in the body is another way to help polarized parts simultaneously unblend. To guide clients through this exercise, invite them to identify two parts (or teams of parts) who are in conflict with each other—where do they show up in the client's body? Then ask the parts if they notice the client. If not, ask if they are willing to notice the client.

Once they are willing, ask which part needs attention first, and guide the client to send breath, or perhaps a thread of light, to that part while saying, "You are not alone." What does this part want the client to know? It may use words or any preferred way of communicating. Do the same with the second part or team of parts. Assert that there is plenty of space in the body for all parts.

End by asking the client how they feel toward these polarized parts now and what they notice in their body.

---

[*] Our conference table exercise adapts a technique developed by Richard Schwartz's early IFS collaborator, Michi Rose.

Other Ways of Visualizing
Gatherings for Polarized Parts

Any image can help polarized protectors unblend if it brings space, clarity, and an opportunity for perspective-taking. We offer some ideas here, but you can also invite clients to think of other options.

- Self sits with polarized protectors at a kitchen table or a banquet table.

- Self and polarized protectors gather around a campfire.

- Self sits on the floor with a classroom of polarized protectors who face each other.

- Self coaches or acts as the referee for polarized teams who gather on opposite sides of a net or a playing field.

- Self conducts an orchestra and polarized protectors are the musicians.

- Self is at a ranch and each group of parts has their own corral.

Externalizing and Personifying Polarized Parts

This exercise inquires into the motives and feelings of polarized parts by interviewing one part at a time. You and the client may be able to cover two parts in one session, but sometimes it's better to focus on just one. Let your intuition be your guide.

To begin, invite the client to place polarized parts in separate chairs (or different spots on a couch). Let the client know that they are going to embody one part at a time. Then ask all other parts, if they are willing, to relax back. If they have concerns, listen to and acknowledge these concerns until they're willing to step back. When everyone is ready, the client can sit in one chair and let that part take over. Then interview this part with the following questions:

- What is your job?

- Why do you do this job?

- What would happen if you stopped doing it?

- What do you want for the client?

- How old were you when you got this job?

- What is it like to do this job?

- Whom do you protect?

- What do you want the client to know?

When one interview feels complete, the client can go back to their original seat and describe the experience. When they are ready, or during the next therapy session, they can do the same for the opposing part. After these interviews, ask the client what they learned. How do they feel now toward the polarized parts?

INTERVENING IN POLARIZATIONS

When firefighters are active, treatment providers tend to view them as the problem and ignore the internal criticism that managers dole out. In IFS, however, we map how each part affects other parts. Although it may take time for the client to map out the relevant pattern, they will recognize the behaviors and feelings they're naming as all too familiar.

When intervening with polarizing parts, we start by clarifying what drives the protectors (e.g., the need to engage in a distracting or soothing behavior versus the need to function and perform in various settings). When these parts are in overdrive, clients can feel confused and alarmed by their extreme rancor and impulsivity. In this regard, two tenets of the IFS model are immediately useful. First, constant conflict between protective parts is inevitable in an addictive system. Second, each team of parts, no matter how offensive, has positive intentions for the client.

For example, Santiago was a forty-two-year-old, Latinx, gay, cisgender high school teacher who first came to therapy for an overriding sense of depression, though he was also worried about his use of ecstasy and alcohol and his increasing impulsive sexual encounters that he considered risky. He had been in therapy for about six months. In this session, the therapist helped him identify his addiction polarity.

WORKING WITH A POLARITY

Santiago: I did it again this weekend. It's pretty crazy. I know I shouldn't go to apartments with strange guys. But I can't stop. When I get high, I don't care.

Therapist: Well, first, I appreciate your sharing this and being so honest. I'm know it's not easy.

Santiago: Yeah, you know I'd rather not discuss this. I mean it's fine to go out. I need to go out and do something besides read eleventh grade English papers. But last Saturday I got really messed up, and then I went with this guy—I guess to his place—which is really not cool of me to do. Why do I keep doing this? The guy was attractive but seemed kind of... a little too pleased with himself. Self-involved. And he drank a lot on top of the ecstasy, which affected his performance, I have to say.

Therapist: Can I reflect back what I'm hearing in parts language?

Santiago: Sure.

Therapist: First, I'm hearing those soothing, firefighter parts who want to get you out of your head. They like to get high, drink, and hook up. They don't care if it's risky for you to be out of it in a strange place with a guy you don't know. They don't think about risks. Is that right? (*Santiago nods.*) And then I'm hearing some other, more cautious parts. Your manager team worries about your safety. They track how often this happens, and they're concerned. Right?

Santiago: Yes. I mean, I'm worried about it. I'm getting fucked up, pardon my French, and it's not great to be out there that way. It's actually depressing, you know? Like, the next day I'm hungover, but also, just in general, I feel depressed. I'm still alone.

> Santiago's manager team speaks out fully.

Therapist: So you're noticing that your mood is also affected. You already felt depressed, but after that night, it got even worse, and you have parts who feel even more alone now. (*Santiago nods.*) I wonder if you would try something with me?

Santiago: What?

Therapist: Visualize yourself at a table, maybe your kitchen table. You're seated at the head of the table. (*Santiago nods.*) On one side, you find all those parts who want to go out and get high—like really loaded—and hook up. Maybe you see them. Maybe you can just sense their energy.

Santiago: I see them standing by one side of the table. They're restless, like they can't sit down.

Therapist: Okay, that's fine. But ask them to stick around for just a bit.

Santiago: They'll stay, but I don't think they'll stay for long.

Therapist: Okay, that's fine. Invite the ones who worry about or feel critical of this behavior to sit on the other side of the table.

Santiago: There are lots of them.

Therapist: Make the table big enough for everyone, and you sit at the head. (*Santiago nods.*) And now just take a breath and see if they notice you. (*Santiago nods again.*) Let them know that you need both sides. That they're all important.

Santiago: The wild ones are skeptical, but they're here. They hear me.

Therapist: Great. And let those worried, critical parts know that they have an important point too.

Santiago: They're not sure they trust me either. But they could use some help on this, yeah.

Therapist: That's fine. Trust takes time! Ask them all to look at you for a minute. You're here to earn their trust and help them. We know they all mean well for you. There's room for everyone.

Santiago: They like the idea of not being alone. They don't really get where this is all going, but they're calmer.

Therapist: Great. Enjoy that calm with them. That's what can happen when you all get together with the intention of listening and learning. (*Santiago nods and sits quietly with his eyes closed.*)

> The therapist focuses on facilitating this Self-to-part connection.

The therapist guided Santiago to notice and connect with both teams—the soothing firefighters and the worried managers. Although the concept was new to Santiago, and he didn't have any expectations about how it would help, he noticed that making a connection with both teams quickly calmed his parts, which was a reinforcing outcome within the session as well as for future Self-to-part connections.

DE-ESCALATING THE MANAGER-FIREFIGHTER POLARITY

As we've covered, manager and firefighter parts live in the same system and share the same desire to keep the system functioning. We don't choose between them; we build relationships with both teams. As critical managers feel understood and calm down, beleaguered firefighters get some relief. The reverse is also true. As firefighters tone down risky behavior, controlling and cautious managers get some relief too. Just as these two teams escalate together, they de-escalate together, and the sense of inner community builds. A client might say, for instance, "It feels good to understand this about myself" at the end of a session. Or they might validate a dominant manager by saying, "I feel sorry for my perfectionist. He never ever gets rest or appreciation." As the client develops warm, collaborative Self-to-part relationships inside, they also gain appreciation for the adaptive intentions of each protective team.

For example, Thea was a twenty-eight-year-old Greek American, partnered, heterosexual, cisgender woman who was currently in graduate school. She reported that she often drank large quantities of wine starting early in the day and also got high on cannabis. Recently, she missed a class she was supposed to teach because she was too intoxicated. Additionally, she was arguing with her boyfriend, Tom, frequently.

DE-ESCALATING A POLARITY

Therapist: I know it's not easy to talk about all this. It sounds like the drinking and getting high are really a worry for you right now, especially since you missed your class.

Thea's Firefighter: Yeah, I mean I've always partied plenty, which is fine. Who cares? But I really got in trouble with my graduate adviser for missing my class. That was pretty fucked up. And my boyfriend is on me now, too, which is pissing me off. Like he's not getting loaded? But I thought, okay, fine, I'll ease off for a while. And I *was* doing really good, ya know? Like even over the weekend. But then I got totally wasted.

> She reports on a firefighter-manager polarity, speaking from both sides.

Therapist: What parts do you notice as you speak right now?

Thea's Firefighter: I guess I'm angry. Like why can't I stop? But really, I just want to be able to drink like other people. Like why do I have to give it up? And I'm mad at my boyfriend. Like now he won't get off this.

Therapist: Sounds like tension is building everywhere. We've been talking about how you have two teams that weigh in about alcohol and cannabis. There's the firefighter team, which wants to drink and get high and do whatever it wants to do. And there's the manager team, which make rules, tries to keep you in line, and says when it's time to stop. And now it feels like your graduate adviser and boyfriend are jumping in on the side of the manager team, is that right?

Thea's Firefighter: Yeah, that sums it up. And I'm, like, sick of Tom nagging me.

Therapist: I hear that, and it feels unfair to you since he drinks a ton as well. I have a question for you, though. Does any part of you sometimes, secretly maybe, see his point? Like, do you have a part who says, just inside in your head, *This is going too far*?

Thea's Manager: Well… Yeah, I do. I mean I don't want to get kicked out of graduate school.

Therapist: So, for right now let's just set aside, for a few minutes, what Tom is saying and go to your parts. Is that okay? (*Thea nods.*) Each of your teams wants something good for you. They have roles in your system—and good intentions for you. Let's check in and ask what they want for you. (*Thea nods again.*) Focus first on the manager side and ask this question: If they could have whatever they wanted, if they were in total control of the universe, what would they want for you?

Thea: They want me to get control of my life. They hate when I fuck up!

Therapist: They want you to do what you're supposed to do, right? (*Thea nods.*) Tell them you hear that. They have a point, right? That firefighter team has been messing up lately. You are listening. You are the one who listens to everyone.

Thea: They didn't realize that. Yeah! I'm not one of those firefighters. They're taking that in.

Therapist: Okay, great. And then, when you're ready, get in touch with the drink-and-get-high team. (*Thea nods.*) How are they trying to help when they get you loaded?

Thea: They want me to have some fun, catch a break. Like, feel better! Ya know?

Therapist: Right. Tell them you hear that. You need to have fun. But what, specifically, do you need a break from?

Thea's Firefighter: The whole routine—my whole life! I'm anxious all the time. Like, I'm really behind and I screw up, so I drink Red Bull and stay up all night, but I'm still never really on top of my game. I feel like hell. Like, I ache all over. I've got no one to help me. I just can't do this anymore. (*She weeps.*)

Therapist: So your firefighter team knows this. They see the worried managers who push you, don't they? You're caffeinated and stay up at night, yet you can't get it all done. They're harsh and critical, and then some parts feel really bad and want to give up. And the firefighter team takes you away from all that, yes?

Thea: (*She nods.*) They shut my brain down.

Therapist: All that noise and pressure—the firefighter team is a relief valve that soothes you. What would they need from you for them to feel okay about easing up a bit?

Thea: They think I'm one of the managers; they don't really see me at all.

Therapist: That's right, they just know those driven managers. Can you validate them, Thea? Yes, there are many driven parts. However, you aren't those parts—you're the calm one who is listening now.

Thea: Okay, yeah, they can tell I'm here. They say they need the managers to ease up and put less pressure on the *shoulds*, ya know? They want me to stop working all night long. They want me to take this Saturday off and ask for a short extension on that lab report. They agree I can wait till later to have a drink.

Therapist: Now check in with the managers. Can they ease up a bit?

Thea: They don't totally trust me, but they get it. They are really tired. They need a break. I'm letting them know we can work on this together. They'll see if it gets better if I don't drink during the day for a while.

Therapist: How does this feel to you, Thea?

Thea: A little calmer! It's kind of scary, but I'll give it a try.

In this example, the therapist guided Thea to validate both teams in her addiction polarity and then brokered a harm-reduction deal where each side agreed to ease up a bit. This truce may not hold for long, but it gave Thea more information about the concerns and compulsions of her protectors. The conversation had not yet gotten around to her exiles, but that would come next.

Welcoming Both Sides of a Polarity

In your mind's eye, seat yourself at the head of a large table. Be sure that you are *there* at the table, not simply looking at yourself from afar. Then bring to mind a firefighter part (or a team of parts) who your managers don't like or trust. This doesn't have to be your most difficult firefighter part. Visualize this part (or team of parts) sitting on one side of the table. Describe how you feel toward them.

_____

_____

_____

_____

_____

_____

Next, think about the manager parts that are in opposition to those firefighters. Invite them to join you as well, sitting opposite the firefighters at the table. How do you feel toward the manager parts?

_____

_____

_____

_____

_____

_____

_____

_____

If you find that either the manager team or the firefighter team is blending with you, ask what they need from you in order to be willing to separate. Reassure them that you are not the other team; you're the one who listens to everyone. How do they respond to you now?

_____

_____

_____

_____

_____

_____

_____

_____

Let both teams know that there's plenty of space for everyone and that you're not trying to get rid of anyone. You're aware that they all have positive intentions for you. Reassure them that neither side will lose if they let you help. Let them know that you're here for both teams. How do they respond?

_____

_____

_____

_____

_____

_____

_____

_____

Are you still at the head of the table, noticing the teams on either side? If so, what is it like for them to be with you without them taking over? What is it like for you?

_____

_____

_____

_____

_____

_____

_____

_____

Instead of glaring across the table at each other, ask each team to shift their gaze and look toward you. Ask them: Would it be good for them if, going forward, they didn't have to do what they do to handle each other? What if, going forward, they were not alone because they all had you to help out? Would they be interested? Describe how they respond to your attention.

_____

_____

_____

_____

_____

_____

_____

_____

_____

Draw Your Triangle

Many therapists in this line of work have had a complicated journey with their own firefighter activity. This exercise helps you identify your inner polarities and clarify the connections between your protective teams and your exiles. It invites you to notice and befriend (have an open-hearted exchange with) all of the parts involved: the firefighter parts who enjoy substances or some other escapist or soothing practice, the manager parts who worry about the practice, and the sensitive exiled parts who are being kept out of awareness. By getting familiar with your own polarities, you get better at spotting and accepting your clients' inner conflicts.

As you participate in this exercise, be aware that anxious managers may feel nervous about letting you connect with a firefighter part who they deem potentially out of control, as if just acknowledging its existence will awaken the dragon and invite a flood of shaming. Remind them that you aren't connecting with firefighters to endorse their behavior. Rather, you want to understand their motives and give them new options. By the same token, the Self can help exiles let go of the sense of shamefulness and feel better.

To begin, identify one of your soothing firefighter parts. You can choose a part who is active now or who has helped out in the past, whichever feels most doable for you. Visualize your part engaging in its favorite activity (or activities)—perhaps lying on a sofa, eating, and watching TV; scrolling through social media with a drink in hand; or smoking cannabis (or nicotine). View this part as if through a one-way mirror. Notice its facial expressions. Is it happy, worried, or checked out? Notice its body language. Is it relaxed, tense, exhausted?

How do you feel toward this part? If you are open, ask it what it wants you to know. If you don't feel open, check in with the parts who are blocking you and closing your heart. Ask if they are willing to unblend and trust you. If they are, continue getting to know your firefighter. How is it trying to help you? What function does it have in your inner world? What is it afraid would happen if it didn't do this job for you? Tell it you're listening. Write what you learn in the *firefighters* box at the end of this exercise.

Next, notice any parts who react to this firefighter. These parts may appear in the form of a voice delivering a message or some anxious activation somewhere in your body. You may notice a controlling manager who wants to limit how much time or money you spend engaged in this soothing firefighter activity. You may notice a judgmental manager who says the firefighter part is morally bad, too risk-taking, or weak. You may notice a worried manager who fears the firefighter part will get out of control or who remembers times when the firefighter did go too far. How do you feel toward this reactive manager? If you are not open, check to see if the firefighter part has unblended thoroughly.

When you are able to feel curious about the manager, ask what it needs you to know. Listen to it closely. What are its concerns? Reassure it that *you* are not the one who is engaging in firefighter behaviors; you are the one who listens to everyone. Acknowledge and validate its concerns—managers often have a good point! What does it want when it comes on so strong? What is it afraid would happen if it relaxed and let you take care of this firefighter part? Write what you're hearing in the *managers* box at the end of this exercise.

Continue by asking each protector who steps forward to describe how it got started in this role. How long has each protector been doing its job? What do they fear would happen if they had to entirely stop doing their jobs? They may express common worries of falling apart, reliving the past, or feeling overwhelmed with shame. Once the protectors have shared their fears, ask them whom it is that they protect. Then invite the protectors to consider this option: What if the Self could take care of the sensitive exiled parts they're protecting? If the protectors agree, ask if it's okay to briefly connect with these exiles. If not, acknowledge their concerns and accept their decision, but ask permission to keep the conversation going and to prove that you could do this safely.

If protectors are willing to step back, welcome and pay attention to the exile. You may see an image of a younger version of yourself, like a snapshot located someplace in your past, or you may simply feel sadness, pain, or the urge to shrink away or hide in your body. Regardless of how the exile shows up, focus on that. Breathe yourself bigger to make room for the part. Let it know that it's not alone because you're here now. What is it like for the exile to have you nearby? How do you feel toward the part now? If a protector shows up, ask it to step back just enough so you can connect again, just for now.

When you feel open again, ask the exile to share one thing that will help it feel understood in this moment. Take that in. If your protectors feel comfortable, spend more time listening to the exile. Pay attention to any sensation of anxiety in your body. If anxious protectors activate, thank the exile for showing up and ask where it would like to go that's safe and comfortable until you can return. Then write what the exile shared with you on the corresponding box marked *Exiles*.

Finally, review the filled-in table as a new map of your parts. Notice each protector team. How do you understand them now? Do they see each other differently? Remind these parts that they don't have to try to fix each other anymore because they can strategize for the good of everyone with you. Point out that you know the exile now, you understand its burdens, and you're here to help. Then send love and compassion to your exile. Thank it for showing up. Appreciate how long it's been waiting for support and how courageous it has been. Let it know that, going forward, you and all these protectors aim to work together to establish safety, and that you will stay in relationship and be available to everyone. No one needs to be alone anymore.

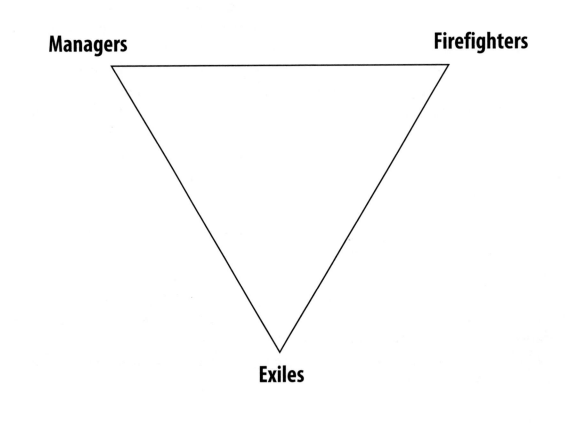

Managers

Firefighters

Exiles

CALMING THE ADDICTIVE POLARITY

As we've been emphasizing, protective parts in addictive systems are in chronic conflict and have no trusted leader. To calm the addictive polarity, we start by identifying, welcoming, and befriending both the functional managers and the risk-taking firefighters. We help both teams separate from the client's Self and talk about their fears, intentions, and addictive processes. The client hears all this for the first time, understands their divided cravings for control and soothing, and sees how they escalate with each other. The client's Self gets traction by developing strong, clear, responsive connections with each part, which encourages them to keep unblending. When a part unblends, clients feel more accepting of themselves and often experience a greater sense of agency: *Okay! Maybe I can do this now.* Parts who feel connected with the Self are more willing to unblend in the future, both in session and at home.

As ranting managers calm down and firefighters let up on high-risk practices, the mind feels more spacious, and parts trust the Self more. At this phase of treatment, we see clients begin to make different choices on occasion. However, these periods of unblended psychic space also give exiles the opportunity to push for attention, which can cause protectors to double back and panic. To head off the urgency of exiles, we continue to include them in brief *one-way* connections to the Self, reminding them they are not alone and that we are coming with help. We promise that addressing the concerns of tough protectors will help to create more space and safety for them. We ask them not to overwhelm the system, which is an intervention Schwartz discovered early on in his work with exiled parts (Schwartz & Sweezy, 2020).

As the client invites protectors to be direct about their worries, they gradually pivot from acting out to saying no, saying yes, and making requests. If protectors believe therapy is moving too fast, we can slow down. These conversations around speed and need are novel for parts who are used to being disregarded and disempowered. They are often crucial turning points in the client's inner journey.

GETTING TO KNOW FIREFIGHTERS

By the time clients with compulsivity problems walk into our office, they will have tried countless times—sometimes with multiple strategies—to control their drinking, eating, sexual obsessions, or online gambling. Some of their parts will be angry about being shamed, controlled, or judged during bad experiences with previous treatments (Hari, 2015). Others will be fearful of failing again or even ready to die before they tolerate one more humiliation. When an IFS therapist is able to notice these negative assumptions and guide these parts to step back, therapy will feel safe for the client and their parts will engage. A firefighter part might start dropping hints, like complaining that other people think their behavior is a getting worse, or a manager might spill the beans more directly. Either way, this information gives us an opportunity to move on from the addiction polarity and review the client's earliest experiments with firefighter behaviors.

We recommend coupling this review with lots of appreciation for a couple of reasons. First, firefighters are remarkably perceptive. They see that the harsh, self-loathing tirades of managers who are trapped in a grim devotion to obligation lead to more loneliness, shamefulness, and despair. Their concerns are legitimate and reality-based. The client's internal environment really is too harsh. In turn, firefighters aim to balance *shoulds*—too much caretaking, too much responsibility, too much shaming, too few resources—with some *wants* that distract from emotional pain and loneliness. However chaotic and self-damaging a firefighter's behavior, it provides real relief. When the client is able to be curious, they learn that firefighters ignore long-term negative consequences because they are upholding one side of a potentially lifesaving (if precarious) bargain.

Second, we make a point of appreciating firefighters because clients have a wide variety of priorities when it comes to change. For example, they may want to work on their bulimia but not feel ready or interested in changing their drinking patterns. As with harm reduction approaches, we subscribe to the idea that recovery is any positive change a client makes (Szalavitz, 2016; Tatarsky, 2007). Our first priority is not controlling compulsivity but getting in relationship and building healthy inner connections between firefighter parts and the client's Self. Additionally, we invite the client to identify how their addictive parts are serving them at this time, and we solicit information about other firefighter activities that feel beneficial, like hanging out with friends, walking the dog, playing an instrument for fun, racing motorcycles, submerging into a novel, bingeing on a TV series, playing video games, or going to a movie.

Since we aim for the client to see their risk-taking behavior in a new light, we recommend pursuing the firefighter review gently. We hope they will learn to understand (rather than be critical of) their addictive behaviors and they will appreciate (rather than fear) the depth of their need for relief. Toward this end, it is important that we head off potential backlash from critical, shaming managers before we do a firefighter review by asking about their concerns. Managers rightfully fear getting friendlier with firefighters. They don't trust the Self yet and assume that firefighters will interpret any rapport as permission and endorsement of what they do. We gain manager trust by responding to their legitimate fears and concerns. To do so, use the following steps.

Ask, Validate, Ask

First, ask inside if any part objects: "Does any part feel worried or object to you talking about your early experiences with me?"

- If a firefighter part fears that the therapist (or another part internally) will judge its behaviors, ask about its intentions ("What would have happened without you?") and validate its sense of necessity.

- If a manager part fears that the therapist (or another part internally) will not judge firefighter behaviors, validate this concern but stand up for the firefighter: "This firefighter part is intense, but not crazy. It tried to help that kid escape a really painful time when no one else was helping."

Next, ask about manager fears: "What would happen if you didn't say critical things right now?" It is important to note their validity of these worries—as managers have seen the past behaviors of other parts. Typically, critical managers have one or all of these concerns:

- The exile will blend with and overwhelm the system.

  - Validate the client's experience of this in the past, and offer to help exiles so they don't need to overwhelm again.

- The firefighter will take over.

  - Validate that firefighters have run the show many times with disastrous consequences, and promise that firefighters are more complex than they seem so they, too, can be helped.

- The manager thinks it *is* the job it does, so it will disappear if the job ends.

  - Validate the manager's hard work, and promise that the client's Self will have no interest in getting rid of any part. You are just offering the part a chance to worry and work less.

- The manager fears that someone else will get mad and reject the client.

  - Validate that the client has been shamed, rejected, or disowned many times before, and promise to support the client's new process not to judge or control anyone.

After reassuring managers and securing their permission to proceed, explore the client's earliest history of substance use or other high-risk behavior. Follow up on hints or direct confessions with nonjudgmental, open-ended questions. Start by inviting them to think of when they first took a major risk, got in big trouble, or felt like they were acting out. Ask out how old they were at the time and inquire about their circumstances.

For example, if the client smoked a cigarette, shoplifted a sandwich, lied to get out of trouble, played cards for money, looked at porn on their dad's computer, started dieting, had sex for the first time, or in some way rebelled more openly, what was going on in their life? How old were they? Depending on a client's environment and history, this rebellion could have happened when they were a teenager, or even in grade school. As they revisit the past, help them connect with their young protectors and listen to their intentions. You will learn the level of risk they faced at home and whether any adult was available to guide or protect them. You may hear about parents, preoccupied with work or with other relationships, who were stuck in their own addictive cycles or who were emotionally, physically, or sexually abusive. You may hear about chronic chaos, lack of supervision, food insecurity, or loneliness.

For some clients, this pain and loss may be more subtle. Their environment may have been quite secure and well-resourced, yet they still felt unloved, were chronically anxious about their performance or appearance, or were always invalidated and thus felt unsafe being assertive. Each client has a story. Whatever their childhood circumstance, they gain clarity by looking at the positive intentions of their parts—whether it was an eight-year-old firefighter part who got entry to the "big kid" crowd by smoking cigarettes; a ten-year-old part who was left home alone, comfort eating junk food in front of the TV; a thirteen-year-old part who soothed their rage at school bullies by cutting their arms and inner thighs; or a fifteen-year-old part who began to boycott food after being humiliated at dinner.

As author Maia Szalavitz (2016) wrote in her book *Unbroken Brain*, "Addiction doesn't just appear; it unfolds" (p. 38). We understand how addictive processes develop throughout a client's life, but when the client listens to their firefighter parts, the big picture comes into focus more clearly before their eyes. They see their childhood vulnerability and understand how it led to the clever strategies of their young protectors. When the client can see how lonesome, neglected, or scared their young parts were, the client has a first shot at self-compassion: *I wasn't bad. I was desperate!*

Firefighter History Review Questions

- Do you remember the first time you tried something risky in your neighborhood? In your home?

- Do you remember ever wanting to get away with something and not get caught?

- How was school? Did you participate in outside activities?

- Who was home when you got home from school?

- Were you ever home alone? If so, where were your caregivers or siblings?

- What did you do when you got home from school?

- Were you able to relax in your home? If so, how did you relax?

- Could you relax in your neighborhood? Did you feel safe outside of your apartment building or home?

- Did you have fun when you were young? If so, what was fun for you?

- Were you ever nervous or scared in your family? At school? Was anyone there to help you with those fears?

- How did your immediate family function? Did your caregivers ever use drugs, drink alcohol, have eating issues, become inappropriate sexually, or get violent?

- Did you feel comfortable being yourself with family?

- Did you feel the need to hide any parts of yourself or to hide any of your favorite activities at home or in school?

- What was your extended family like?

- Did you have responsibilities at home? If so, at what age?

- Did you have enough food to eat? What kind of food was it?

- How old were you when you started to diet, gamble, use substances, or engage in other risk-taking behaviors? What was happening at the time?

- Are you hearing anything critical about your young self who _____ (e.g., got high, smoked cigarettes, looked at porn)? If so, what is the critical part afraid would happen if it didn't say these things right now?

Expect that many clients will be disconnected from their needs and motives when you conduct a firefighter review. This might be the first time they notice their childhood vulnerability. That's because, as we've learned, many clients who are engaging in addictive practices come from chaotic or disengaged family systems and learned to disconnect from their needs at a young age, a state that grows over time. As a result, they are not versed in self-care and self-attunement, and they don't easily associate early deprivation and wounding with their addictive process. For example, they don't realize they got high yesterday because they felt overwhelmingly isolated. They don't realize they restricted their food intake over the weekend because they were overtaken by a deep feeling of shamefulness and sense of alienation. Rather, they're most likely to say they had a rotten week and simply felt like giving in to the urge.

Although we might conclude that these clients are avoiding reality and accountability, they are not aware that they are making choices to manage their discomfort and pain. Rather, they report not thinking at all. They're genuinely mystified by their compulsivity and impulsivity. The behavior happens to them— again and again—and they don't see the larger context for their actions.

So how can a therapist intervene effectively when a client has so little self-awareness and sense of self-agency? We start by asking questions that invite clients to notice their patterns and protector polarities. We continue by painting the big picture, pointing out that their protective parts are divided into two opposing teams, and helping them notice how vulnerable they were when they turned to distracting and self-medicating.

To see how this looks in practice, consider the example of Sonia, a thirty-two-year-old, African American, single, heterosexual, cisgender woman, who came to therapy because, as a newly minted nurse, she had an urge to steal drugs on the job.

WORKING WITH YOUNG PROTECTORS

Therapist: You mentioned things were not great at home when you were young. Do you remember how old you were when you first tried alcohol?

Sonia: Eleven. We took beers from the fridge in the neighbor's garage.

Therapist: Is that also when you started smoking cigarettes?

Sonia: I was ten when I started smoking. Me and this kid in my neighborhood would go to the park and smoke his mother's cigarettes. Sometimes we played around, too. We didn't really know what we were doing. But I guess it was kind of nice just being together.

Therapist: It was good to have company. What else was going on when you were ten and eleven years old?

> The therapist validates and inquires about her environment.

Sonia: My dad left and my mom was depressed. She stayed in bed. She was drinking, though she thought we didn't know. She hid the booze in a boot in her closet.

Therapist: And what were you and your younger siblings doing?

Sonia: Mike kinda moved in with the family next door. That left me with little Pete and Mom. I begged for money from relatives in the neighborhood and did the food shopping and took care of little Pete. Sometimes the lady across the street left containers of leftover food on our doormat. And when little Pete got burned, I took him to the hospital.

Therapist: How?

Sonia: I picked him up and ran. Then the government people came. That was when we went to foster care.

Therapist: Sonia, when you talk about this, what do you hear inside?

Sonia: *You let little Pete get hurt. You let those people take him away.*

> This is Sonia's critical manager team.

Therapist: Did you and your brothers go to the same foster placement?

Sonia: We did. But Mike snuck out of the foster home and went back to his friend's house. They let him stay there. Then Aunt Caroline took little Pete, and I eventually went back to Mom.

Therapist: When did you go back?

Sonia: After about a year, I think. She got sober for a while.

Therapist: So you have a part who says little Pete getting burned and the government people coming to take you all away was your fault.

> The therapist introduces parts language.

Sonia: It was. But then I got a boyfriend, Marty, when I got home. He was sixteen. I was fourteen. We had fun while it lasted. He got vodka from his older brother who worked in a liquor store. (*She shrugs.*) What can I say? I was a bad kid. I dropped out of school too many times to count. It was a miracle I finished.

Therapist: Your critical part sees that kid on her own and says she was bad. Let the part know that she wasn't bad. I'm hearing she was a kid in the worst kind of circumstance. She had all that responsibility and no grown-ups to help. She was too young to keep her little brother safe. Goodness! She needed someone to take care of her. Then she got put in a stranger's house, she was all alone, and she blamed herself. She needed some comfort and relief. Cigarettes were a start, but Marty and alcohol were even more effective.

Sonia: (*She tears up.*) I never saw little Pete again. I begged my aunt to take me too, but she said she couldn't.

Therapist: And what did the critic inside you say when that didn't happen?

Sonia: *No one will ever love you. You're a selfish, nasty girl.*

Therapist: Does the critic still say stuff like that? (*Sonia nods.*) What is it concerned would happen if it stopped?

Sonia: (*She hangs her head.*) I'd be too much.

Therapist: And?

Sonia: And no one would ever love me.

Therapist: Do you agree, Sonia? (*She nods, looking at the floor.*) Okay, so let the critical part know that, yes, there was a young girl who had all that responsibility and no grown-up help. Her mother was ill, and she tried to keep her little brother safe, but she was too young. Who was taking care of her? She was vulnerable too. She was alone and scared, and she had a critic beating her up inside. (*pausing*) Can you see her in that foster home?

Sonia: I see her… She's sad.

> This is the exile.

Therapist: Is she aware of you? (*Sonia nods.*) Let her know you're here now. Would she like your help?

Sonia: Yes.

Therapist: Tell her we'll come back to her soon. First, we have to check in with the parts who drank and smoked and so forth to get their permission. Can you see them too?

Sonia: I see the fourteen-year-old. She needed Marty and the booze.

> This is a firefighter part.

Therapist: Do you get that she needed Marty and the booze? (*Sonia nods.*) Would she like your help too?

Sonia: Yes.

Therapist: Okay, great. We'll come back to her.

Since Sonia was convinced that she was bad as a child (and was still bad now), it was clear that her judging, critical managers were still present. At the same time, she felt unlovable, so her exiles were also in her consciousness. This is a formula for firefighter intervention that can lead to a recurrence of compulsive behavior. While many clients like Sonia can readily, even dispassionately, recount a devastating family history, we should not mistake that dispassion for calm and self-compassion. Their protectors have no idea how to meet the needs of traumatized, abandoned parts. In IFS, we assert that it's never too late to heal attachment wounds and bring exiles to a safer place. We make sure firefighters have a chance to explain their good intentions, and we validate the legitimate cravings of exiled parts for comfort, warmth, adult protection, and safety.

ASKING ABOUT OUTSIDE INFLUENCES

Many clients trying to control their addictive processes are subject to external pressure from loved ones. Their behavior is chaotic, they habitually disappoint others, they lack follow-through, and they have legal and medical problems. All this recruits the manager parts of friends and family, and also of the health care professionals who cycle through their life trying to help. All of these well-intentioned people (including us!) explain, shame, threaten, manipulate, beg, and nail down contracts in which the client agrees to minimize or stop the addictive behavior. However, this external pressure won't end the chaos, stop the cycle of self-destruction, or effect a cure. In contrast, it will motivate firefighters to resist intervention and act out more stridently.

Of course, some clients have family members or partners who are more troubled, chaotic, and self-destructive than they are, in which case therapy needs to help the client create new boundaries and support parentified or desperate young parts. This is particularly true in families that have little or no apparent interest in recovery, where the client faces wrath, derision, or exile if they choose a more settled, manager-led life. While distressed families deserve an equal measure of compassion, the client has an obligation to free their parentified young rescuers from an impossible task.

Our job is to help clients explore their relational network, including outside pressures and obligations, so we can clarify external polarities that activate and impact their compulsive behaviors. How does the client spend their day? Whom do they see? What are those relationships like? What we often find is that a client's firefighters are polarized with the manager parts of a partner, a parent, or some authority figure, which bolsters their determination and hinders the client's access to manager parts.

QUESTIONS FOR CLIENTS ABOUT OUTSIDE INFLUENCES

- How much does _____ know about your substance use (or bulimia, gambling, or other patterns of compulsive behavior)?

- How much information do you feel safe sharing with them?

- What do you *not* want to share with them?

- What are you afraid would happen if they knew everything?

- Have their opinions or feelings about this behavior changed over time?

- Do you and _____ argue about this compulsive behavior?

- Does _____ have a compulsive habit that worries you?

- When _____ complains about your behavior, how do you respond?

- How does your response impact the relationship?

- If your relationship with _____ was good, what would it look like?

- Do you and _____ engage in this behavior together? If yes, what is that like for you?

- If you stopped this compulsion, how would that impact _____?

- If _____ stopped their compulsion, how would that impact you?

- Have you shared your vision or plan about your addictive behavior with _____?

- Do you know what plan or vision _____ has for their compulsive behavior?

- Do you feel you can speak honestly with _____ about your plan?

- Do you have fears about the relationship ending if you make changes?

BEFRIENDING MANAGERS

If you aren't already engaging in shuttle diplomacy between firefighters and managers as you complete the firefighter history review, it's important to go back to the manager team. Negotiating with these more socially astute parts may seem counterintuitive, but their shaming is what motivates firefighters to engage in compulsive practices. Therefore, if managers calm down, firefighters are much more likely to cooperate. As you turn to managers, your first aim is to befriend them, which requires understanding their motives and concerns. Here is a rundown of what you need to know about managers.

1. **Managers take care of business.** This team puts the highest value on task completion and personal effort. They work diligently to maintain stability, they strive to meet the client's relational needs, and they revere personal growth. They encourage people to take on new challenges, and they foster maturity. However, their desire for progress can turn them into pitiless critics when they fear life is careening downhill.

2. **Some managers are dedicated to self-sacrifice and self-denial.** When clients are blended with these types of parts, their attention is permanently fixed outward. They are always trying to discern the needs of others and oversee the welfare of someone else—anyone else!—but themselves. They sacrifice for partners, children, parents, bosses, and coworkers. These manager parts often began their job at a very early age, in homes with nominal parents who were too preoccupied with their own addictive

practices to take care of anyone. When we help the client notice and listen to these parts, we find out who the caretaker part is protecting, and then we can validate its generosity and devotion.

3. **Managers can be extreme.** Once a client's system is entrenched in addictive processes, managers become ever more unyielding. Inner critics, judges, perfectionists, caretakers, logical thinkers, and minimizers take over and keep the client afloat by operating from the neck up. They aim to accomplish basic tasks and mute vulnerable emotions like sadness, loneliness, and despair. They sling contempt, express disgust, insist on perfection, magnify every broken intention as a sin, and stigmatize firefighter compulsions to the nth degree.

4. **Managers reflect the larger culture.** They soak up moralistic, culturally propagated fears about firefighter behavior. These attitudes make a tremendous contribution to their bias against firefighters, who they view as immoral, destructive, and in need of harsh discipline (Hari, 2015; Hart, 2021). They condemn the character of firefighters with little attention to their motives and no interest in asking why. But despite their vitriol, managers mean well. Their biases come with the job of protecting exiles and go when the job ends.

5. **Managers have good intentions and reasonable fears.** They are allergic to chaos, insecurity, failure, and humiliation. Their fears run on two tracks: (1) Firefighters will get out of control and take over (*You'll use again. It will ruin everything. We'll lose our job!*), and (2) the system will be overwhelmed by the emotional pain of exiles. As a result, they work diligently to silence emotional pain and control firefighters. In a balanced system, however, they get real satisfaction from fulfilling expectations at work and in relationships.

Once you understand their motives and characteristics, you can befriend managers. We believe direct access is a good option for engaging overly responsible, frantic, shaming, and blaming managers. We simply ask them how they are trying to help. In addictive systems, critical managers are typically trying to prevent more of the chaos that firefighters engineer, but they struggle to see that firefighter parts are well-intended. When we say something like, "I hear how parts of you hate the using," they may reply, "No, I really hate it! I hate those out-of-control parts." If we ask these parts to move aside, they feel insulted. Therefore, we believe it is most effective to engage them by normalizing and validating their perspective: "Right, of course you don't like it." We ask about their massive reform efforts and validate the pride they felt when they could make the changes stick. At the same time, we promise them that we can help those stubborn firefighter parts if they will permit.

After engaging with the manager team, we review and highlight the addiction polarity with metaphors. For example, we may describe how managers are trying to take charge in a classroom of unruly kids or keep a boat afloat in stormy waters. We underscore the impossible nature of their balancing act with firefighters, with each side escalating and no one seeing the exit ramp. We commiserate with managerial exhaustion. We promise that exiles who are behind the scenes can be helped.

Next, we help managers unblend by asking the client how they feel toward the manager. Curiosity, kindness, compassion, and a collaborative stance are the golden keys to manager cooperation. They want relief from isolation, oppressive responsibilities, and fears—and an assurance that we are not trying to replace them. Managers like control. They do not want to leave their post when all hell could still break loose. If we appreciate their strengths and promise not to hamper them, they are more likely to accept our support. We ask them to consider, "What if you didn't have to handle this alone? What if the Self could help with the risk-taking firefighter parts?"

Throughout this process of befriending, we interrupt manager rants as they arise. When a shaming, contemptuous manager takes over, we interrupt its tirade promptly and guide the client to notice its harsh language. Even parts who rant repetitively in sessions are just doing their job. We point this out, acknowledge the part's ability to do its job well, and ask it to take a break and be more direct. Would it be willing to tell us exactly which part it feels the need to attack? What does it fear would happen if it stopped going after that part?

In addition, we help managers understand firefighter behaviors. Before firefighters are willing to speak for themselves, we explain to managers that firefighters are more complex than they appear. Managers know all the pain, stress, disconnection, and loss the client has faced. We insist that firefighters have always aimed to relieve or divert from that pain and stress. And we say that the Self, *the one who listens to everyone*, is now here to help.

Finally, we invite the manager team to plug into a new paradigm. They know their hard work has backfired over and over. They know that shaming evokes shamefulness and vulnerability, which feeds right back into that firefighter craving to soothe and medicate. They like the Self's patience and persistence, so we suggest a new way of doing things. What if instead of wrestling firefighters to the floor, managers allowed the Self to invite firefighters to the table where they can all break bread? What if instead of shaming firefighters, managers allowed the Self to offer the firefighter parts a safe haven and help the exiles they protect?

As we model this new way of being, we ally with managers. To this end, it helps to let them know two things: (1) *No one can control you.* If managers decide to let the Self help out and don't like the results, they can always go back to their old job and do things their way. (2) *Firefighters have equally thankless jobs and feel equally stuck.* Just as a couple therapist needs to gain the trust of both partners to bring the temperature down, the client's Self keeps getting in the middle of the addiction polarity—redirecting protective parts away from their old roles and asking them to bring their concerns to the Self.

The following case example illustrates how to befriend a manager. Gina was a forty-six-year-old, Romanian American, divorced, heterosexual, cisgender mother who lived with her teenage daughter in a Midwest suburb. She came to this session worried about her increasing use of cannabis. As it turned out, her inner critic was concerned about much more than cannabis.

Befriending a Manager

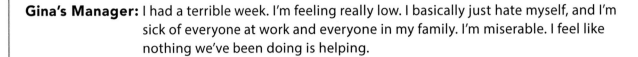

Gina's Manager: I had a terrible week. I'm feeling really low. I basically just hate myself, and I'm sick of everyone at work and everyone in my family. I'm miserable. I feel like nothing we've been doing is helping.

Therapist: Oh, that does sound miserable. I'm sorry it's been so tough! I hear that you're just miserable. Or I might say it this way: I hear that you have parts who feel just miserable. When your parts are feeling miserable, yeah, it feels like nothing is getting better.

Gina's Manager: It's not getting better. It's really not!

Therapist: Yeah, I hear you, it feels like nothing is going right. Can you tell me more about what's been especially tough this week?

Gina's Manager: I forgot to do some important things at work because I'm an idiot. So, when I picked up my daughter, I was distracted, and then we got into a huge fight because she was being selfish and wouldn't listen to me. Then when she stopped talking to me and was holed up in her room, I decided to get high. The next morning, I felt like hell when I woke up. I couldn't believe I just gave in like that. It was so stupid!

Therapist: That is a lot.

> The therapist stays neutral and interested.

Gina's Manager: And now I'm back to getting high every day. Sometimes all day! Which I hate. I was doing so much better a few weeks ago.

Therapist: Weed has had a starring role this week. I know that can feel scary because the urge to use was down before. Can I reflect all this back to you in parts language? (*Gina nods.*) I'm hearing that it's been painful at work and at home this week. And that the part who helps you get away from all that by getting high keeps offering you a break from the pain and stress. At the same time, your critic is having none of it. No excuses! It is just angry and hostile about you using cannabis so much again. Is that right?

Gina: (*Gina nods.*) Yeah, I guess it really is mad.

Therapist: So let's pause for a moment and take a few breaths together. How is it to hear that version of the week?

Gina's Manager: (*Gina closes her eyes.*) Like I said, I'm miserable. I hate that I keep doing this. (*She wipes away tears*)

Therapist: You mean the critic hates that the cannabis-using part has upped the ante like this, right?

> The therapist highlights the manager-firefighter polarity.

Gina's Manager: Yeah, it's like I'm back to square one.

Therapist: Hmm, yes. The critic says you've made no progress at all, not if you're using like this! Does the cannabis-using part pay attention to the critic?

Gina: Yeah. And it disagrees!

Therapist: They do disagree. I wonder if that vulnerable, lonely exile is absorbing all this. How is she feeling?

> The therapist asks Gina to notice the effect of polarized protectors on the exile.

Gina's Manager: I don't know. I'm so depressed.

Therapist: It can be hard to separate out. How about if we just listen to the critic for a minute? (*Gina reluctantly nods.*) How do you notice the critical part right now?

Gina: It's a furious voice in my head all the time.

Therapist: Can you hear it right now? (*Gina nods.*) Okay, let it know that you hear it and that you assume it has a very important message for you. Would it be willing to tone it down a little so you can hear the message better? We don't want it to go away, just ask it to give you enough space to listen. That way, it can also notice that you're listening. Tell it that you are the one who listens to everyone.

Gina: Okay. It's a little quieter. Not much though! It's just surprised to hear that I'm not the one getting high.

> Gina describes a little unblending.

Therapist: That's right, you're the one who's here to listen. Ask how it's trying to help when it goes after your cannabis-using part.

Gina: It says that part is screwed up and out of control as usual. It will never quit. This has to stop! And I'm just getting worse. I keep messing up at work. And things with my daughter aren't good.

Therapist: Do you see its point? (*Gina nods.*) The cannabis-using part did step up when another part panicked about work. And the critic also seems upset with the part who got angry when things blew up with your daughter. It can get busy with all these parts! But reassure the critic that you are the one who listens. Let it know that you see how vigilant it is with any part who is not doing the right thing.

> The therapist guides Gina to validate and stay in the middle, without taking a side.

Gina: It hears me.

Therapist: What is it afraid would happen if it didn't hammer out these harsh messages all the time?

Gina's Manager: That's obvious! My life will go totally off the rails. I'd fall apart again.

Therapist: We don't want that. How are you feeling toward the critic right now, as it tells you about its big job? It has all these other parts to watch and try to control.

Gina: I see how much it has to do! It never rests.

> Gina is getting access to the perspective of her Self.

Therapist: What if it didn't have to do all this alone? What if you were in its corner and you two could help these other parts as a team?

Gina: It says it doesn't think I can handle it. I've never handled it before!

Therapist: Well, that is true. Stuff really falls through the cracks sometimes. But when that happened, it wasn't you. Other parts do run the show sometimes. What if, going forward, the critic didn't have to handle those parts all alone because you took on the big job of helping them?

Gina: Well, it says it would be fine if I do. But it has huge doubts.

Therapist: Of course. Trust takes time and evidence. Do you want to stay connected and build that trust? (*Gina nods.*) Would the part like to have a relationship with you and see how you'd handle those parts?

Gina: Yes. It wants help. It is actually exhausted. It would be good if I could somehow help those parts. (*She sighs audibly.*)

Gina arrived at therapy feeling miserable after a week of dropping the ball, being on edge, arguing with her daughter, and using a lot of cannabis. In IFS parlance, she had a *parts attack*. As her protectors escalated, she felt out of control again. When she used impulsively after a tough day, the critic went on the warpath in a thankless effort to shame her firefighter part into reforming. Unfortunately, this amplified her exiles' sense of worthlessness and motivated her firefighter to lean more heavily on the calming effects of cannabis. Since the critic's desperate efforts to control the firefighter were making matters worse, the first order of business in this session was to help it feel less alone and more connected to Gina's Self.

As Gina illustrates, we can facilitate dialogues with insistent critics. First, we ask them how they're trying to help. Critics in addictive systems typically want to prevent more of the chaos and disasters that firefighters engineer, which is surely positive. As the manager team unblends and develops an ongoing, trusting connection with the Self, we can guide the client to ask some pointed questions, ever so lightly and with affection. As hard as these managers work, have they managed to fix or even discourage firefighters? The client often gets a rueful acknowledgment that their tactics haven't worked, so plan B might be a good idea. As this path opens, the client turns their attention back toward firefighters with the curiosity and calm of Self-energy.

QUESTIONS THE THERAPIST CAN ASK CLIENTS ABOUT THEIR CRITICAL MANAGERS

- Where does this critic show up in the body?

- What kind of energy does it have? How does it feel?

- Do you see it? If so, what does it look like?

- Do you hear it? If so, do you hear it inside or outside, and what does it sound like?

QUESTIONS CLIENTS CAN ASK THEIR CRITICAL MANAGERS

- Which part(s) are you attacking?

- Which parts worry you most?

- When you go after _____ part, how are you trying to help?

- What would happen if you stopped going after that part? Have you seen that happen before?

- What if firefighters are more complex than they seem? If you saw there was another way to help this firefighter so it used its energy in a better way, would that give you a break?

- If we could retrieve exiles and they could let go of their burdens, would you still have to work so hard?

- What do you want to say to me?

- How old are you?

- How old do you think I am?

- What would it be like if you could do this with me and didn't have to handle it alone?

REORIENTING BACK TO FIREFIGHTERS

As the client refocuses their attention back to firefighter parts, they might find that some are so walled off they seem to be on autopilot. Clients may believe that the urges and compulsivity of these parts hinder them from trying new options. In reality, though, these parts are not incapable of negotiating, nor are they permanently unreachable. They just haven't been reached yet. We can engage them with direct access.

For example, Ida was a forty-four-year-old, Polish American, single, cisgender woman who first came to therapy to curb her drinking. Her father had been chronically ill since she was a child, and Ida had been his main caretaker. She reported a pattern of working feverishly for 10 to 12 days at a time and then spending a week or so holed up in her house, drinking nonstop. When Ida was working, she usually showed up to therapy, but whenever she was drinking, she always canceled. She was worried about her health but felt unable to change her drinking habits.

The therapist invited her to identify the central polarity between her manager and firefighter teams. Her driven, compulsive manager team included a workaholic part, some driven caretaker parts, and a team of harshly judgmental critics who shamed her for drinking. Her manager crew was balanced by a compulsive firefighter team, which included a very committed drinking part, a rebellious angry part who felt like life was unfair, and a group of defensive parts who studiously avoided hearing feedback about her compulsive drinking and work habits. She had a few memories and some awareness of having been lonely when she was a child, but she had no genuine access to her early experiences and described herself as emotionally shut down.

Reorienting to a Firefighter

Therapist: We've been focused on the big polarities in your system, and we've seen how inner battles keep you feeling stuck. You've talked with some harsh, shaming managers who have given you some space, which is great! At the same time, we're not so connected with the part who is committed to drinking. We could just invite that part to be with us right now. She's always welcome in our sessions. If she came here with you, we could get to know her.

Ida: You mean I should show up here drunk?

Therapist: Well, I'd still like to be able to talk with you and her. But yes, I'm serious about inviting her to visit with us, drunk or sober. She has been shamed and hidden for so long. I want her to feel welcome.

Ida: (*She laughs and shrugs.*) Well, okay, maybe I'll do just that!

Therapist: No driving drunk, though, right? An Uber or a taxi. (*Ida nods.*)

Two weeks later, Ida showed up at the session and said she'd been drinking. The therapist welcomed the drinking part and lauded her courage for showing up despite a long history of having been judged. Ida said her drinking part wanted to talk with the therapist directly, which is what we call explicit direct access.

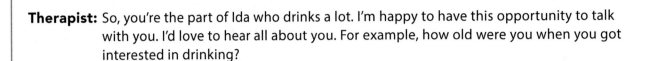

Therapist: So, you're the part of Ida who drinks a lot. I'm happy to have this opportunity to talk with you. I'd love to hear all about you. For example, how old were you when you got interested in drinking?

Ida's Drinking Part: Thirteen. Me and my girlfriends sat up one night drinking a handle of vodka from the liquor cabinet in this one girl's house. We put it in orange juice and 7UP—and it tasted great! It was the first time I ever had fun. We laughed and ran around the house and acted crazy. It was a blast. I was sicker than a dog the next day, which was awful, but I knew I'd do it again as soon as I could.

Therapist: Uh-huh. It sounds like you were able to forget everything and just be wild kids, is that right? (*Ida nods.*) And it was unusual for you to have fun with friends.

Ida's Drinking Part: Oh yeah, my dad was so sick. He was bedridden my whole childhood with one thing or another. Since my mother hated taking care of him, it was up to us. We came right home from school and got him to the bathroom. I knew he was waiting. It was kinda terrible.

Therapist: Mm-hmm. So much pressure on Ida to be responsible. So you were the part who helped her get a little down time, be a little lighthearted, and act like a kid.

Ida's Drinking Part: I guess I was! Otherwise, it was just depressing. So hopeless. Nothing to look forward to—like ever.

Therapist: Right, so do you think there were some even younger or more tender parts who felt hopeless about anything ever getting better?

Ida's Exile: I'm still hopeless.

> Ida is now blended with the hurting, hopeless exile, along with the drinking part.

Therapist: Right, yes of course. You've felt hopeless for a long time. It's like it never goes away. We're going to help you. But I wonder if you could be patient for just a little longer. We need permission from the drinking part first. Is that okay?

Ida's Exile: Okay.

Therapist: Great. Thank you. So now I want to talk with the drinking part again. (*Ida nods.*) I wonder, as the part of Ida who drinks, if you're aware that drinking keeps that hopelessness quiet?

Ida's Drinking Part: Well, I know if she didn't drink, she'd be miserable.

Therapist: Right. You've been protecting Ida from feeling hopeless and miserable. I know it would be tough and scary to stop. Your help has been essential! But now if Ida could help that hopeless part so it felt stronger and not so alone, would you get a break?

Ida's Drinking Part: I guess so. But I'm not sure anyone can help.

Therapist: Right, you'd need evidence of that. Ida and I would need to show you. And, with your permission, we will.

This session informed Ida about the benign intentions of her drinking part and opened her heart to its feelings. It also introduced her to a key exile. While it is unconventional to invite a client to come to—or stay in—a session while engaging in their compulsive behavior, it can serve to reassure parts quickly and powerfully that we mean what we say: All parts are welcome. We won't judge.

WHEN FIREFIGHTERS RUN THE SYSTEM

Keep in mind that the line between a firefighter and a manager gets blurred when the client's functioning is very compromised at the far end of the addictive continuum. At this extreme, the addictive process becomes a proactive, rather than a reactive, activity. The craving for pleasure or escape gives way to the need to maintain the habit or to avoid feeling sick. The client now must find a way to engage in the compulsive activity—such as locating money to score drugs or pay for their next sexual encounter—in order to properly function. To do so, firefighters assume the proactive role of managing the client's days—hour by hour, minute by minute. They can be impressively and disturbingly resourceful about lying, stealing, and dealing. As consequences pile up, including those that are physical, emotional, legal, and relational in nature, they just work harder to avoid the obstacles—anything to engage in the activity.

When the client is in this circumstance, we need to be more proactive as well in terms of helping them find a safe environment. If we feel we need to advocate for more intensive treatment, like a residential inpatient program, we are honest and transparent with the client about this. We acknowledge up front that many parts are not interested in listening to our message. We speak to abandoned, fragile parts about being cared for and safe, and we let manager parts know that external containment measures will give them a break.

When we take this route, protective firefighter parts can rant aggressively and contemptuously, accusing us of abandonment or betrayal. In this case, we will probably need to help our own managers stay calm so we can guide the client to hear from the parts inside who do want to survive—who yearn for health, safety, and freedom from compulsion. We may want to tell the client that we believe they have the internal resources to feel whole, steady, and at peace. As the client considers intensive treatment options, we are a supportive resource and we stay available (if possible) as the client completes the inpatient stay or intensive treatment program. Here is an example.

Lukas, a 34-year-old, Lithuanian American, single, gay man, had recently left his job in retail and returned to live with his mother in her home. She set Lukas up in therapy, reporting deep concerns about his daily drinking, drug use, and angry outbursts, which she called dangerous. At the time of this session, the therapist had been seeing Lukas for a few months. He acknowledged his mother's concerns and identified some manager parts who agreed with her and others who didn't like living with her, which meant he needed to find another job. These parts were polarized with the firefighter parts who loved using and didn't think it was all so bad. They said his mother drank a lot as well and shouldn't judge him.

Lukas said he started using in high school, attended local college sporadically, and felt okay with working in retail when he still had the job; he left his previous position after he was upset over a relationship ending badly. All his friends drank and took pills regularly, and he said he couldn't imagine not using. He had recently shown up late and missed a few appointments, and this week, he reported having an intense fight with his mother after she accused him of stealing. He had been sleeping on a friend's couch.

Working with a Proactive Firefighter

Therapist: You look pretty exhausted.

Lukas's Firefighter: I am. I just got home, and my mother went crazy on me because I was gone for a couple of days. It's none of her business what I do. She's nuts anyway!

Therapist: She called me and left a message saying you took money from her. That sounds pretty intense and miserable. If you took money from her, she doesn't have much.

Lukas's Firefighter: She called you?! What the hell, I didn't steal from her! She's always on my case—

Therapist: (*Therapist interrupts.*) She sounded pretty clear. Can you tell me more about what happened the last few days?

Lukas's Firefighter: My friends and I got fucked up, what else do you want to know?

Therapist: Your drinking and drugging parts took over for a few days. And it sounds like another part of you took money from your mother to make that happen. (*Lukas sputters.*) Lukas, you don't have any income these days. It sounds like your using parts got desperate. So why did you come home?

> The therapist invites the other parts to speak up.

Lukas's Firefighter: I didn't take money from my mother! (*The therapist doesn't respond.*) I don't know why I came home. I wanted to get out of there. I guess I needed sleep.

Therapist: Okay. And you made it here to your appointment. So can I reflect back what I'm hearing? (*Lukas shrugs.*) Your using parts ran the show for a few days. To serve their agenda, another part who, based on what you've been showing me, has amped up lately, took some money from her. (*Lukas opens his mouth to protest again.*) Let me finish! And it will not admit to doing that because other parts of you are dismayed.

Lukas's Firefighter: Whatever.

Therapist: This binge has affected your body. You're exhausted. And it has affected your mood. You're screaming your head off with your mother, which has also been happening more—

Lukas's Firefighter: I told you, she's a drunk. Where does she get off calling you?! She just wants me to be home with her—

Therapist: (*Therapist interrupts gently.*) Yep, your mom has some real issues of her own, no question. Let's leave her out of it for now, okay? I'm more interested in your perspective.

Lukas's Firefighter: My perspective is you should leave it alone, too. I'm fine. I don't need this shit from you, either.

Therapist: I got it. I know your partying parts couldn't care less what anyone else thinks or feels. I also get that in their own way, they help you. You like being with friends, and when you're high, you feel better. I get that. And I also see you are here, in my office, at your appointment. I know that some of your parts have said they want more in life than just using. Your partying parts are taking more risk now. They will do just about anything. But I also see other parts in action. You've also tried to help your mom sometimes. And you're a good friend. And you've got parts who have been through tough times. No dad, kids bullying you, being in the closet. I know you've been through a lot. So, I'm wondering if there are also maybe one or two small parts, who feel, even briefly, pretty worn out, worried, or just tired of the craziness. Like you could use a break?

Lukas's Firefighter: I could use a break from all this bullshit!

Therapist: I hear your angry part who wants to defend you. I understand that a lot of your parts do not want to listen to any of this. I also know that you really wanted that relationship to work out, and you were heartbroken. You've had to be strong on numerous occasions. I know your partying parts give you a break. And I know there is more to you that just using and getting fucked up. Speaking for my drug counselor parts, I'm just going to focus on the using right now and say I am worried. I know you're frustrated with your mother, but she does care about you. The stakes are getting higher, and I see parts getting involved in stuff that you don't even want to admit, like stealing. I'm sure I don't know all of it, either. In my experience, those parts make sure you have the means to get high but, in the end, you feel even worse about yourself.

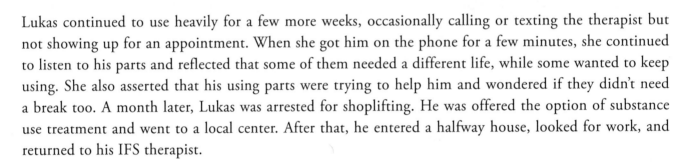

Lukas's Firefighter: I am fine, you don't need to worry about me. This is bullshit! I'm leaving.

Therapist: Of course, you can leave. Since my parts are worried about you, I'm texting you the name of the treatment center we talked about, just so you have it. I know the people there. They have a couple of different programs that you could check out. Like I said, the stakes are getting high for you and you're taking bigger risks now. I care about you, and I'm not alone. I understand that many of your parts don't want to stop using, which is what they would want you to do at the treatment center. And I know that you have other parts who want a break. It doesn't have to be this hard, Lukas. There are other ways to go. You can text me. I am happy to keep meeting with you, or you can text the center, where you could get a break for a while. (*Lukas walks out, slamming the door.*)

Lukas continued to use heavily for a few more weeks, occasionally calling or texting the therapist but not showing up for an appointment. When she got him on the phone for a few minutes, she continued to listen to his parts and reflected that some of them needed a different life, while some wanted to keep using. She also asserted that his using parts were trying to help him and wondered if they didn't need a break too. A month later, Lukas was arrested for shoplifting. He was offered the option of substance use treatment and went to a local center. After that, he entered a halfway house, looked for work, and returned to his IFS therapist.

After returning to therapy, Lukas and his therapist interviewed his using parts, and they identified these parts' clear desire to take him away from or medicate his abandoned, wounded exiles. He was curious about recurrences and discovered that his using parts had a message for him about exiles who needed attention. He learned that his using parts wished he would be more autonomous when his caretaking, compliant managers worked to avoid conflict with his mother or with certain friends. He also got connected to an LGBTQ+ Alcoholics Anonymous (AA) group, which gave him a supportive new social community.

By listening to every one of his using parts, Lukas was able to create his own vision for the future. Some of his parts were in alignment with the AA commitment to sobriety from alcohol, but he did have other parts who still wanted to smoke cannabis and relax with friends occasionally. Because of his occasional cannabis use, no one would sponsor him, but he did discover other AA friends who were not wedded to AA's clean and sober mantra and who were experimenting with their own version of a productive and balanced life.

EXILE INTERVENTIONS

Whenever clients focus internally, they can get flooded with the warded off memories and feelings of exiles, which is called an *exile jailbreak*. In response, firefighters will activate instantly. They may distract (for example, through dissociation), or they may start hunting for some way of soothing (*I want chocolate!*). Meanwhile, managers will get anxious and start to criticize. Our job, as Schwartz says, is to be the eye of the storm. Accordingly, we ask protectors to let us reassure the exile and negotiate with it to be patient.

For example, Irina, a thirty-five-year-old, Slovenian American, partnered, gender-neutral person, first came to therapy for posttraumatic stress disorder and chronic restrictive eating patterns. In past sessions, most of their protectors would agree to unblend, but then a dissociative part would promptly blend whenever they approached young exiles. This left Irina unable to focus or respond to questions. In this session, the dissociative part finally agreed to refrain from taking over, and Irina started to hyperventilate.

INTERVENING FOR AN EXILE

Therapist: Are you there? Hi, Irina. I see that a panicked part has taken over. I'm going to talk with it directly. Are you there? (*Irina nods.*) Would you like help? (*Irina nods.*) Great. You're welcome here. We want to help you. Here's what you can do to make sure we can help you. Are you listening? (*Irina nods.*) Great. Give Irina a little space. If you let them in, even just a little, they can help you.

> The therapist uses explicit direct access to connect with a panicked exile.

Irina: (*They shift and begin to look calmer.*) Okay.

Therapist: How's that?

Irina: Better.

Therapist: How do you feel toward this panicked part now?

Irina: I'm glad I can breathe now.

Therapist: Does it hear you? (*Irina nods.*) And how do you feel toward it?

Irina: I want to help it.

> Irina now has access to their Self.

Therapist: Ask what it needs from you.

Irina: Attention.

> Irina's protectors hear that the exile only needs what Irina is actually capable of providing. This will calm them.

Therapist: Is it willing to be patient while you negotiate with protectors so that you can give it the attention it needs? (*Irina nods.*) Great. What does it need to seal the deal right now?

Irina: It needs to know that I'll be back.

Therapist: We will not forget. You will be back. Would it like to go to a safe place to wait for you?

Irina: Yes.

Therapist: Help it find the right spot, Irina.

Irina: Okay.

Therapist: You've got it?

Irina: Yes.

When protectors are not ready for an exile to tell its story but the part blends anyway, we have to intervene. We speak to it directly, negotiating with it to unblend and promising that we won't forget to give it the attention it craves. At the same time, protectors have the opportunity to see that exiles have an agenda too, and that they won't overwhelm the system if they get what they want.

One-Way Connections with Exiles

Exiles can appear early in treatment in subtle ways that befit their position on the backburners of consciousness. For instance, they often pop into a client's current narrative and divert the client's attention to the past. Say the client is reporting a stressful incident at work when, without preamble, they pivot to an earlier time (...*like when my father left and my mother fell apart...*) with no awareness of the memory's significance.

When an exile pops up like this, we pause, notice, and make the most of this connection opportunity by inviting it into the session. If the client has enough Self-energy, we may guide them to tell the exile that we won't hear its whole story now but that we know it's important and we are aiming to hear it as soon as all parts agree. We don't want to pursue these trailheads vigorously before protectors are ready, but the contact can be warm, even if it's brief. Success in therapy depends on connecting with these parts safely. If it feels right, the client may want to ask, "Is there is one thing, just for today, that you want me to know about you?"

In addition, when we sense the client is feeling vulnerable but hasn't noticed, an exile is probably making an appearance. In this case, we might say something like, "We've been discussing your relationship with your partner and his recent drug use. You haven't mentioned this yet, but I'm sensing a sad part underneath your frustration. Is that possible?" We can then invite the client to pause and focus internally. If the client insists that they do not feel the sadness, we let it go for now. If they do notice the feeling, even just briefly, we guide them to let the part know that they feel it and are aware of its presence.

As the client connects with their sad part, an image may appear, or the client may simply feel the sensations that go with sadness. Again, if there is enough Self-energy, we guide the client to stay with the sad part a little longer and have a short exchange. We guide the client to ask it not to overwhelm the system so that protectors will trust it and give it a real chance to be heard. If the sadness does start to flood the client, we can ask the exile what would happen if it unblended instead. Exiles often overflow the dam because they fear being put out of mind again. They don't trust the Self yet, and they assume a full-on deluge is their only way of being noticed. As therapists, we must work with our own parts to stay present and connected—helping the client validate the exile's fears while asking for cooperation and promising to return.

 We can then direct a client to identify how and when this vulnerable exile first made its appearance. (*I was feeling angry and sad about my partner using drugs all the time, and then I remembered how sad I was when my dad left.*) Then the client can track their pattern—feeling sad, lonely, ashamed, and so on—and notice how those feelings connect to present-day actions. Since protectors are terribly afraid of exposing exiles to more judgment and injury, they need to feel good about the Self before they will allow a full connection between exiled parts and the Self. Observing moments of one-way connection— tendrils of contact between the client's Self and the exile that establish a template for safe relating— allow protectors to grow more comfortable, which sets the stage for the exile to tell its story when the time is right.

To see how this looks in practice, consider the case of Graham, who was a fifty-two-year-old, Scottish American, heterosexual, cisgender father of two sons who were in college. He described his deceased mother as being chronically depressed and his father, who was now in a nursing home, as authoritarian and punitive.

After immigrating to the United States from Scotland as a teenager, Graham attended university, pursued a career in software development, and got married in his twenties. He also developed a serious preoccupation with pornography around this same time, which had escalated over the years and included regular visits to massage parlors. His wife divorced him three years ago due to ongoing arguments about his porn use and her suspicions about the massage parlor visits, which he had been denying.

Graham had since chosen to attend 12-step meetings and attended an online support group with the stated intention of staying sober, as they called it, from pornography and massage parlor visits. He reported feeling okay with these expectations but still struggled with feelings of loneliness and shame. As of this session, he had been in therapy for about six months.

A One-Way Connection with an Exile

Graham: I've been really down this week. I've got a deadline at work and there is so much pressure. I went to see my father who, as usual, was terrible to me. He is a miserable man. I don't know why I go. I guess my manager part says I have to see my father.

Therapist: Sounds like that part is trying to do the right thing, but it comes at a big cost. Being around him is really hard on your more sensitive parts.

Graham's Manager: He's a mean person. He yells at the nurses all the time. He criticizes me constantly. You know, I never told him about the porn or anything, but it's like he knows. The other day he told me that the divorce was my fault and I drove her away!

Therapist: It's hard to spend time with him, yet you remain loyal. Is that confusing? (*Graham nods.*) Let's check on these parts. You mentioned one who says you have to see your father, and then you have others who always feel hurt by him.

> The therapist names his polarity between parts who feel alienated and a loyal young parentified part who wields a lot of power.

Graham: Yeah, let's do that.

Therapist: Take a few breaths and focus inside on the part who says you have to see your father. What does it say?

Graham's Manager: I owe it to him. I can't leave him there all alone.

> This is the parentified young manager.

Therapist: And how do you feel toward this part, Graham?

Graham's Exile: I don't like it. I feel trapped.

Therapist: That is another part. It feels trapped and sounds more tender.

Graham: When I was a boy, my father used to come to the table where I did my homework and stand over me. Sometimes he would grab my papers and scream at me that I was no good and didn't work hard enough.

Therapist: Wow, that's rough. And you were so young. The boy is showing this to you? (*Graham nods.*) Can you see him?

> Graham's exile has started to show his experience and Graham has enough Self-energy to continue safely.

Graham: He's terrified.

Therapist: Let him know that you see him. Back then your father was big and scary. But the part doesn't have to stay in that time. He could be with you if he prefers.

Graham: He sees me.

Therapist: How do you feel toward him?

Graham: I feel bad for him. He's little.

Therapist: Ask him to look at you and let him know you care about him. Your heart is open.

> The therapist facilitates the Self-to-part connection.

Graham: He likes that.

Therapist: Let him know we can't hear his whole story today, but we do want to hear it, and we'll keep coming back. Is there one thing he wants you to know right now?

Graham: (*He listens intently.*) He was trying so hard to make his father happy. But he was always scared.

Therapist: Are you taking that in? (*Graham nods.*) He tried hard. We will come back to him. Would he like to wait someplace safe till then?

Graham: With me.

Therapist: Great. Keep him with you.

Graham: He wants to curl up under a blanket and sleep in my bedroom.

Therapist: Perfect. Now take a moment to shift back to the manager part who says you have obligations to your father. Did it observe you helping the boy?

Graham: Yes. It's calmer now.

Therapist: Great. Thank it for stepping back for now and trusting you to reach out to that vulnerable little boy.

Graham: Okay, yeah. It wants me to take care of the boy.

In this session, Graham became aware of an exile, and his Self connected with this exile's protectors, which helped him feel more stable. Managers and firefighters all need ongoing reassurance that the Self will show up and be reliably available to vulnerable parts. Graham's case example includes a common IFS intervention called a retrieval (Schwartz & Sweezy, 2020). Notice that Graham invited his young boy to wait someplace safe until they could connect again. Utilizing imagery to invite a vulnerable part to exit an emotionally charged or dangerous scene and settle in a safer location is a surprisingly effective means for increasing inner system stability and forging trust with the Self. Offering a brief, but successful, one-way connection paves the way to develop a fuller two-way relationship.

Two-Way Connections with Exiles

A one-way connection introduces the exile to the Self and helps the exile see that the Self is not a protective part. The Self might simply say, "Hey! I'm here, I care, and I want to get to know you better." A two-way Self-to-exile connection, on the other hand, is more complex. As protectors have repeated experiences of feeling validated by the Self and understood (*Maybe I can actually count on someone inside to pay attention and be supportive!*), they are able to relax for longer periods of time. This gives the exile a seat at the table. Communication flows better and the Self has the opportunity to demonstrate that it is a stable, steady resource.

As protectors see the Self in action and step back, the exile becomes bolder about speaking for its needs. With the Self as a witness, the exile experiences a long period of connection, sometimes lasting more than one session, which offers what the part has always needed: compassion, safety, and validation. This, in turn, brings optimism and hope. Building the client's capacity for more complex inner connections is like strengthening a muscle. Consistent Self-to-part connections create a new template and boost trust in the Self throughout the internal system.

For example, Jamie was a forty-five-year-old, single, lesbian, cisgender, Irish immigrant. She worked as a teacher, lived alone, and had not been in an intimate relationship for many years. She had always seen herself as overweight and reported that she had been struggling with overeating and depression since her mother's death the previous year. She had built good connections with her team of inner critics who had long been polarized with her comfort-eating part.

While therapy was helping her feel less depressed, she still went into what she called an "eating trance" in the evening and on weekends. She had identified an eight-year-old comfort-eating firefighter—a girl who liked to hide in the pantry and sneak snacks. She was a very young protector who had been rejected and shamed by her mother's inner critics and her own inner critics for decades. In therapy, Jamie had helped her critics ease up quite a bit, but not entirely. They were still protecting another eight-year-old part—a sad, neglected little girl in a lot of pain. In this session, Jamie established a two-way connection with both eight-year-olds.

A TWO-WAY CONNECTION WITH AN EXILE

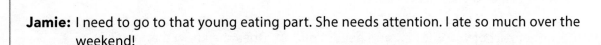

Jamie: I need to go to that young eating part. She needs attention. I ate so much over the weekend!

Therapist: Sounds good. As you spoke about eating over the weekend, were you seeing the comfort-eating part? Or can you feel her in some way now?

Jamie: Well, I feel the critic who is so disgusted with the eating. But I get it! I understand why she's worried about eating that much. She hears me. She's stepping back.

Therapist: Okay. Do you see or feel the girl who wants to eat?

Jamie: I see myself standing in my kitchen with bags of chips and dip and stuff.

Therapist: Great. Let her know you see her.

Jamie: I'm telling her that I'm here and I see her.

Therapist: How do you feel toward her?

Jamie: I feel bad for her. She seems kind of desperate.

Therapist: Show her that you care, in whatever way seems right. (*The therapist pauses.*) Ask if she's willing to talk with you.

Jamie: Yes. She's sick of being in the kitchen.

Therapist: Invite her to be somewhere else with you. (*Jamie nods.*) And if it feels right, let her know she can bring a snack with her.

> The therapist suggests that Jamie welcome the firefighter as she is, without asking her to change.

Jamie: Really? That's okay? (*Tears well up in her eyes.*) She can't believe it! She can't believe it's really okay to eat with me. She's bringing the chips.

Therapist: How do you respond?

Jamie: I'm telling her it is okay. She is okay and I'm good being with her—and her food!

Therapist: That's right, you care about her.

Jamie: (*She speaks after a period of silence*) She's only eight years old.

Therapist: How is she trying to help?

Jamie: She comforts me. She knows I'm lonely.

Therapist: Another part of you is lonely and needs comfort. Does she know that part?

Jamie: Yes. It's actually another eight-year-old. Her mother watched TV and ignored her.

Therapist: Can this girl see you?

Jamie: Yes. I see her and she sees me. I feel so bad for her. She's filling her face. She needs that food so bad, but she is afraid of being caught!

Therapist: There are two girls, right Jamie? The sad, lonely one and the one who protected her by binge eating for comfort.

Jamie: They're twins.

Therapist: Would they like you to be in the pantry with them? (*Jamie nods.*) They're safe with you. Can they feel it? (*Jamie nods, teary.*) I see the tears, Jamie. How are you doing?

Jamie: It's good to be with them. But I feel sad for them, too. I guess they were sad all the time.

Therapist: Let them know you feel their sadness and desperation. What do they want you to know about that time?

Jamie: They couldn't help it. They loved hiding in the pantry. It smelled good and felt cozy. Her mother didn't want her eating in there. She'd get furious and go off, so they were always afraid of getting caught.

Therapist: They needed the comfort of the pantry and the food. Eating made the sad, lonely one feel a little better, but their mother was scary. Take some breaths together so they feel you being with them.

Jamie: They're feeling me. This is different.

Therapist: Thank them for being willing to take this chance with you. Shall we put the pantry somewhere safe so their mother can't rag on them? (*Jamie nods.*) Where should it be?

Jamie: The moon.

Therapist: Okay. Put them and the pantry on the moon and tell them you'll be back. Can you stay in connection with them this week? (*Jamie nods.*) Great. Arrange that.

> The therapist invites the client to set up a retrieval for the young girls, relocating them to a safer location.

Jamie: (*She pauses, then nods.*) They feel a bit better. They see that maybe I can help. They're relieved.

Therapist: Yes. The comfort eater has been working hard all by herself to protect the sad one. What if, going forward, the sad one could count on you to be there?

Jamie: They're not totally sure about that. They like being together.

Therapist: Right. Of course. We don't want to separate them if they want to be together. Would they like us to come back? (*Jamie nods.*)

Jamie's compassionate connection with this young, protective comfort eater paved the way for an equally strong connection with the lonely eight-year-old. If we listen, young protectors and vulnerable exiles can tell us just what they need. A client's concerned managers—and sometimes a therapist's caretaking parts as well—tend to worry that exiles have near insurmountable pain and therefore need some kind of massive intervention to feel better. In fact, exiles need exactly what they needed when they were hurt: a loving, attuned connection with a dependable, courageous guardian.

Creating Safe Connections with Exiles

A One-Way Connection

The one-way connection, which includes a firsthand experience of warmth, acceptance, and connection, introduces the exile to the Self and demonstrates that no strings are attached. For many exiles, this experience is novel. Some are immediately relieved, while others are skeptical. They see that the Self is different from protective parts and their controlling or distracting agendas. The Self offers kind attention, the opportunity to belong, and the promise of ongoing support. Every Self-to-part connection increases stability within the system. As the Self-to-part bond strengthens, it develops into a more complex, two-way street relationship. To begin creating a safe one-way connection with an exile, invite your client to try the following:

- Identify a vulnerable part.

- Guide a connection to the Self via imagery or activation.

- Check for Self-energy and reassure the part that it is not alone anymore.

- Send care and compassion to the part.

- Let the part know that you can't hear its whole story now.

- Ask the part what it wants to share just for today.

- Reassure the part that you will return.

A Two-Way Connection

A two-way connection between the Self and exiles is free-flowing and trusting. The exile shares important stories and is, in turn, nurtured by the Self's validation and acceptance. In order to unburden, the exile may just need to share painful experiences and feel validated, but if it's stuck in the past, it will need the Self to come back to that time to do what it needed someone to do for it then. With each interaction, the Self earns more trust and license to lead. To begin creating a safe two-way connection with an exile, invite your client to try the following:

- Identify a vulnerable part.

- Guide a connection to the Self via imagery or activation.

- Check for Self-energy and reassure the part that it is not alone anymore.

- Send care and compassion to the part.

- Invite the part to share whatever it is holding.

- Witness and honor the part's experience.

- Spend time gazing at, reflecting with, and embracing the part.

- Reassure the part that you will return.

WITNESSING AND UNBURDENING

Clients in therapy who are addressing extensive periods of substance use or other compulsive behavior may have episodes of intrusive imagery or sensations that relate to traumatic events in the past. These images and sensations often reflect exiled parts who are breaking through consciousness in an effort to get help. These parts have been burdened with bad memories, shocking feelings, and negative beliefs as a result of the traumatic event. Many of these beliefs have to do with being irreparably damaged, unlovable, shameful, or disgusting. These negative beliefs can operate unconsciously for decades, profoundly affecting the individual's view of themselves and the world. As a result, they show up in client stories repeatedly.

Sometimes a client's protectors will see the Self as just another part who doesn't have the capacity to tolerate exiled pain, causing their fear to shoot up whenever the client approaches an exile. They seem to be checking: *Are you really ready for this?* However, the reality is that the client's Self *is* ready to step in and reverse negative judgments about the part. It is ready to witness the exile's story, validate its experience, and assert its inherent value and lovability. When a client is Self-led, they show up alert and open-hearted, and exiles get the sustained care, understanding, and protection they've always needed. As a result, they let go of distorted perceptions about themselves and the world. The client who is present and compassionate to their own story will be liberated to know what they know, feel what they feel, and speak honestly without self-attack.

In this Self-led state, the client—and, if the exile wishes, the therapist—can bear witness to the exile's story through a process known as *witnessing*. Here, the exile may want to show or tell the Self about its experiences in detail, taking the Self to see a seminal scene; it may summarize its experience; or it may just say, "You know all this, I want to get out of here." In this portion of therapy, which occurs within the security of the therapeutic relationship, the exile is the director who guides the Self through its story, rather than reliving it in the same traumatic way. Our job is to stay fully present to the exile's story and do whatever it wants. Along the way, we prompt the client to acknowledge the exile as needed: "Let this sensitive part know you hear it" or "Let this college kid inside know you are paying attention and it is making sense."

In addition to being a compassionate witness to the exile's story, we have two main jobs as IFS therapists. The first is to be what we call a *parts detector*, who calms any protective parts who interrupt the story. If a protector is very anxious and keeps interrupting, we kindly but firmly ask it to step back and assure it that the exile only needs what it has always needed: a safe, secure, loving, and available relationship with someone they trust, and we are in the process of meeting its needs.

The second is to guide the client through the *unburdening* process by following these simple steps. First, we ask the exiled part if it needed help in the past. If so, the client's Self can go back and do for the part whatever it needed someone to do at the time, in a process known as a do-over. This trip through the past with the Self disconfirms the exile's negative beliefs about its identity. When the part is ready to leave the past, we invite it to come to the present and ask if it has burdens from that previous experience. If so, we invite the part to let go of those burdens or, if it is not yet ready to let go, to put the burdens in storage. If the part is ready, we ask how it would like to let its burdens go and suggest releasing them to one of the elements (light, earth, air, water, or fire*), or in any way other that feels just right. Finally, we ask the part what it wants to invite in once the burdens have gone out, and we ask protectors to notice the new state of the now-unburdened former exile. Unburdening is the ceremonial capstone of witnessing.

THE THERAPIST'S ROLE IN WITNESSING AN EXILE AND HELPING IT UNBURDEN

Guide the client as they:

1. Offer to go back and help the part in the past.

2. Offer to help the part leave the past when it is ready.

3. Ask the retrieved part if it has burdens once it reaches the present.

4. Witness the part as it lets go of its burdens.

5. Help the part put its burdens in storage if it's not ready to let go.

6. Ask the part how it would like to release the burdens (light, earth, air, water, or fire).

7. Ask the part what it wants to invite in once the burdens have been released.

8. Ask protectors to notice the former exile who is now unburdened.

The following vignette is a good example of a client's Self bearing witness and joining with an agonized young part (and an exiled angry protector) in the past and making room for a do-over. At the time of this session, Margot was a twenty-nine-year-old Canadian American, single, bisexual, cisgender woman who had been coming to therapy for oxycontin and fentanyl use and posttraumatic stress disorder. During treatment, she had helped some bullying manager parts to calm down and some drug-using firefighters to find new roles. Now she was finally ready to help a four-year-old exile who was being molested by her father in the basement of her childhood house. The therapist and Margot had connected with this part in the past for many brief moments, letting her know she wasn't alone and that help was coming, and Margot had even taken her to a safe place. But she had discovered through flashbacks that the part was back in the basement again.

---

* IFS borrows from the shamanistic tradition of unburdening to the elements to help exiles complete the process of leaving the past and letting go of limiting, painful beliefs about who they are. Michi Rose, an early collaborator in the development of IFS, introduced this feature of unburdening.

Unburdening an Exile

Therapist: Margot, can you see or sense the four-year-old now?

Margot: Yeah, I see her. I feel panicky and sick.

Therapist: Okay she's a little blended. Is it too much, or can you just let her know you're aware of her and we're here to help?

Margot: Uh, okay, yeah. I let her know we're here. But I feel the panic.

Therapist: Right, Margot, such a scary, awful place for this little one. You're feeling her feelings.

Margot: Yeah, she's scared shitless. She feels sick and I do too.

> The exile is blending and beginning to overwhelm Margot.

Therapist: Of course. Let's take a breath together. (*They take breathing pause.*) Let her know that you feel her feelings and you're still here. You're just telling me about her.

> The therapist pauses to facilitate enough unblending to continue safely.

Margot: Yeah. Okay, yeah. I'm here, we're here. Wow, is she panicking!

Therapist: How are you feeling toward her as she panics? Are you with her, or is the panic overwhelming?

Margot: Yeah okay… (*Her breathing slows.*) I'm okay. I'm here for her.

Therapist: Does she want to leave that place?

Margot: She does! She sure wants out!

Therapist: Okay, bring her to the present. She can be with us here or anywhere that feels safe.

Margot: Okay, she's here with me now. She's all curled up.

Therapist: Okay, let's pause, and send her your energy and breath. Let her get used to being with you now. (*The therapist pauses.*) She never has to go back. That time is over, and she can stay with you.

Margot: Right, yeah, okay. She's doing a little better. (*She leans back in her chair.*) She's happy to be with me.

Therapist: Okay, great. How are you feeling toward her?

Margot: Sad. He was terrible.

Therapist: Share that with her, Margot. Help her take in that you get it. Your heart is open to her. You know how hard it was for her to be captured by him.

Margot: Okay, she's moving closer to me.

Therapist: Great, stay with her. Let her feel you. When you're ready, ask if she needs to show or tell you anything about that time.

Margot: She says he hurt her, touched her. She was scared. She feels sick that she couldn't get away from him. (*She begins to get teary.*)

Therapist: Can you keep going? (*Margot nods.*) Let her know you're taking this in. Of course she felt sick and scared and wanted to escape. Does she feel you still?

Margot: Yes. She's showing me. (*She pauses.*) It happened too often. There's a lot. She hated him.

> The exile returns to show her experience from the safety of the present.

Therapist: Of course she did. What does she need from you right now?

Margot: Just to show me.

Therapist: Okay. Can you stay with her? (*Margot nods.*) When she's ready, ask what that was like for her.

Margot: It was like his sickness got into her. (*She slightly curls over.*) I've always felt it in my gut.

Therapist: Let her know you feel it too. Would she like you to come to that time and do for her now what she needed someone to do then?

Margot: She wants me to tell him that he can never, ever touch her again! He's a sick motherfucker. He can rot in hell! I'm sure that's where he is.

Therapist: Here's an angry part.

Margot: Yeah, this part could rip him to shreds.

Therapist: Of course she could. (*The therapist pauses.*) Does that part object to you helping the little one?

Margot: No. They both want my help. I'm putting him out of the house. He's never getting his hands on her again. (*She takes a long pause.*) Yeah, he won't say it, but he's sorry. He knows something is wrong with him. He killed himself, so duh.

Therapist: (*The therapist pauses again.*) Do they feel you there with them?

Margot: Yeah.

Therapist: How is the little one doing?

Margot: She's glad I got rid of him, but she's back there again, curled up on the floor.

> The exile has gone back to the past.

Therapist: Is his sickness still in her? (*Margot nods.*) Okay. It doesn't belong to her. If she doesn't want it, she can send it out.

Margot: She can't believe that. Anyway, she doesn't know how.

> The exile has not successfully unburdened, which is why she returned to the past.

Therapist: I understand. It has been in her a long time. But since it's not hers, it can't stay if she wants it out. We can help with that when she's ready.

Margot: She says fine. Make it go!

Therapist: First we have to ask, are any of her other parts attached to it? Does any part of her want her to keep on carrying his sickness? (*Margot shakes her head no.*) Okay. Then she can send it out to one of the elements: light, earth, air, water, or fire. Or some other way if she prefers.

Margot: She wants the light of heaven.

Therapist: Great.

Margot: Okay. She steps into the light. Me too. I'm going with her. His sickness is like swirling ink in her gut, but the light is getting in to us now. (*She breathes evenly, cries a little, and holds her stomach.*) The light just draws it out… Oh wow, there's more.

Therapist: Take your time. (*They both take a long pause.*)

Margot: That's better. Now she's standing up, stretching her arms.

Therapist: What qualities does she want or need going forward? She can invite anything.

Margot: She wants innocence. She is not him; she is her.

Therapist: Innocence.

Margot: She's lighter, taller.

Therapist: How does that feel?

Margot: Perfect.

Therapist: Does she want to show you anything else, or want anything from you before we finish?

Margot: She's good. She wants to play with my dog, Tucker.

Therapist: Did the angry part see her sending the sickness out? (*Margot nods.*) Does she need anything from you before we stop?

Margot: She saw. She sees me. She's relieved. She wants to come and stay with me too.

> Now the exile can leave the past for good.

Therapist: Excellent, Margot. I'm so glad they're with you now.

In IFS therapy, we invest in befriending protective parts and getting their permission to help exiles first, then we go to the exiles. Generally speaking, protectors take more time and evoke more frustration and intolerance in the therapist (requiring us to notice and help our parts on a regular basis), while exiles evoke more empathy (which can also be a trailhead if the therapist's empathizer is an exile), but it takes far less time once the therapist has access to their Self. It is the essence of acceptance to love fragile, wounded parts in ourselves and others.

Most clients with addictive processes, especially those with early traumatic experiences, struggle to know and accept themselves, with good reason. It's daunting to peer behind a phalanx of protectors and witness injury and insults from the past. These protective parts got into addictive processes to manage despair, and going back to the injured parts who are still in despair can feel like a bridge too far. Protectors don't want to face those terrible experiences with burdened young parts again. In the unburdening process, we befriend protectors and let them know that this difficult job no longer needs to fall on them. The Self can take charge instead. We say, "This isn't your job. Stay right here while the

Self goes back to help that injured part and fetch it out—and then we'll help you too." The following example illustrates how this can look in practice.

Greta was a fifty-six-year-old, German American, married lesbian with a long history of substance use and other addictive behaviors. Her practices include drinking alcohol, taking amphetamines and various tranquilizers, and bingeing and purging. She worked with her wife, Carrie, at a high-powered firm and functioned well enough at work, but Greta felt chronically anxious and depressed and wanted to stop engaging in these self-destructive behaviors. Although Carrie accepted Greta's substance use and bulimia, Greta still hid some of the behaviors from her.

BEFRIENDING A PROTECTOR

Therapist: How is it going, Greta?

Greta's Firefighter: Another crazy week for me! Work is a fiasco. I'm like a hamster tied to a wheel. It's frigging depressing.

Therapist: Mm-hmm. Sounds hard. I hear your managers have come through for you again, which is great. But it also sounds like all that hard work is costing you some.

Greta's Firefighter: Well, if you mean I'm miserable, yes, I am! I can't sleep and I'm not eating right. So, I'm back to Valium. And I had some drinks and whatever. Then I was up eating at 3 a.m. So, all in all, I'm a mess.

Therapist: The firefighters are out in force to help. How does it feel to talk about that?

Greta's Firefighter: Work is hell. I can't sleep. So what am I gonna do?

Therapist: Right, I get it. I have an idea, though. How about we check in and see if we can connect with the firefighter team right now?

Greta's Firefighter: I don't know. I mean, I know why I'm doing it. I just need sleep!

Therapist: Right, there are some obvious reasons, for sure. Your managers are overworked and require help to settle down on the weekend.

Greta's Firefighter: (*She nods.*) Yeah, like I'm responsible for Carrie's entire workload while she's on maternity leave. And her job is above my pay grade for God's sake. I'm not supposed to be responsible for some of these things. I have no experience and I'll get blamed if I make a mistake. Which I'm bound to do.

Therapist: I get it. You need a break! In this circumstance, if I hear you right, the firefighter team is a bit more intense than usual? (*Greta nods.*) And that worries you?

Greta's Firefighter: Well, it's depressing. I don't want to go down this road again. But what am I gonna do?

Therapist: Right. It feels like there is nowhere else to turn. They get the job done! But I do think we could learn more about what exactly gets them so ramped up if we ask. They're doing a little more than just helping you relax, if I understand correctly.

Greta's Firefighter: (*She shrugs.*) Okay, okay.

Therapist: So, Greta, visualize these soother parts in action. Visualize whatever happened on Saturday. (*Greta is quiet.*) Can you see them? (*Greta nods.*) Where are you?

Greta: I'm in my bedroom. I've got the wine, I took some Valium, and I'm watching TV.

Therapist: Okay, this the main soother part. How do you feel toward her?

Greta's Manager: She looks deranged. I hate that I'm into Valium again!

Therapist: She's struggling. I hear that. And did you hear your judging part just now?

Greta's Manager: Yes. I do judge her. She's totally messed up. I can't even look at her. (*She opens her eyes and looks at the therapist.*)

Therapist: I know it's hard to see how checked out this part gets. (*The therapist pauses as they breathe together; Greta is tearful.*) I hear a part who feels sad about all this. (*Greta nods.*) So acknowledge the sad part. Of course she's sad! Would she give you space to hear from the soother? (*Greta frowns.*) The soother is very alone at those times, isn't she? (*Greta nods.*) You could help her, if the critic lets you. (*After a pause, Greta nods again.*) Let her know you see how alone she was on Saturday. But right now, she's not alone. You're there too.

Greta: (*She breathes a little more easily.*) She hates being alone.

Therapist: Let her know you get that. (*The therapist pauses.*) Greta, ask the soother what she's really after when she takes a lot of Valium. How is she trying to help?

Greta's Firefighter: She just wants me to get fucked up!

Therapist: Okay, got it! She wants you to get fucked up. But why now? What's going on now?

Greta's Firefighter: Because I'm always on. I never let up. I never stop worrying.

Therapist: Does that make sense to you? (*Greta nods.*) Let her know you get that too. And, also, that you are not the one who never lets up. There is a part who never lets up, for sure, but that's not you. And you're listening to her.

Greta's Firefighter: Okay, well she's not so sure about that.

Therapist: How do you feel toward her right now?

Greta's Firefighter: I feel good. She's good for me.

Therapist: Tell me more about the good feeling.

> The therapist uses implicit direct access to talk with the soother.

Greta's Firefighter: Well, I feel like, yeah, I do need a break. I do need to feel relaxed once in a while, so what?

Therapist: Your body relaxes and you get that "who cares!" feeling that comes from being high. You can let go. And it's a relief?

Greta's Firefighter: I'm just saying it's not such a big deal. Who cares?

Therapist: You are the soother, right? You're reminding Greta of what's important about letting go. You help her.

> The therapist switches to explicit direct access and speaks to the soother about Greta in the third person.

Greta's Firefighter: (*She laughs.*) I guess so.

Therapist: Greta, can you feel some gratitude for the soother? She finds ways to give you ease. She helps you let go and not worry so much. (*The therapist pauses.*) What is she afraid would happen if she didn't do this for you?

Greta: She thinks I'm a nervous wreck all the time, which is true.

Therapist: Right. Is she helping with anything else?

Greta: She says I don't feel good about myself and that I'm depressed. This job is just a total drag. They're using me and they'll never promote me.

Therapist: So the soother is aware of the part who doesn't know how to defend herself, is that right?

Greta: Yeah, that happens to me all the time. That's my life story!

Therapist: If we could help the part who gets hurt feel stronger and safer, would that be good for the soother?

Greta: Yeah, yeah, of course. If we could, that is. I mean, it's like my whole life.

Therapist: I know. She got hurt a long time ago and you keep getting hurt again. But if the hurt part had you taking care of her, would it help?

Greta: Yeah, it might.

Therapist: Will the hard worker and the soother let you do that? (*Greta nods.*) Okay, Greta. Let her know you're here. Tell her you know all about her and you want to help.

Greta: Wow. She's little!

Therapist: How old?

Greta: Around three.

Therapist: Does she see you? (*Greta nods.*) What does she need?

Greta: Me.

Therapist: What needs to happen?

Greta: I'm picking her up. She needs a hug.

Therapist: How do you feel toward her?

Greta: I love her.

Therapist: Does she need your help back then or is she ready to leave?

Greta: She wants me to tell her mother to back off and stop scaring her.

Therapist: Okay. Invite her mother's higher Self in to help her mother understand.

Greta: Yeah. Her mother needs a lot of help.

Therapist: And what does she need?

Greta: She wants to send her mother away and come with me. She wants to bring her baby sister. Is that okay?

Therapist: Whatever she wants. She's the boss.

Greta: She came to the present. We have the baby.

Therapist: Does she have any burdens from that time?

Greta: What do you mean?

Therapist: Ask her to check. Any feelings from that time that don't change, or beliefs she doesn't need anymore.

Greta: Oh yeah! She thought something was wrong with her.

Therapist: Is she ready to let that go?

Greta: Yes.

Therapist: She can give it up to light, earth, air, water, or fire. Or any way she wants.

Greta: Fire. We're burning it. The baby has some slime on her body. We wiped it off and we're burning the rag.

Therapist: How does that feel?

Greta: Light, fresh.

Therapist: Now what would she like to invite in that she'll need going forward?

Greta: She wants to play.

Therapist: Great. Invite the spirit of play and freedom. (*After a pause, Greta nods.*) Is it okay now to check back with the soother? (*Greta nods.*) How is she doing?

Greta: She's standing up. She looks more together. She wonders if this will work.

Therapist: What does she need?

Greta: She'd like to be free, too, but she's not sure.

Therapist: If she were sure and she felt free, what would she rather do?

Greta: She liked to relax, ya know? She likes the beach, lying in the sun, jumping in the water. I grew up near the beach.

Therapist: Sounds great. Maybe she'd like to watch you with the three-year-old this week and then decide if it would be safe to take a break at the beach.

Greta: Yeah. She likes that idea. But she wants me to find a new job.

Therapist: What do you think?

Greta: (*She nods thoughtfully.*) I think she's right. It's time.

However painful their experiences, exiles revive when they get what they need: a secure relationship with a trustworthy, responsive adult. Protective teams can spend years being convinced that a fragile exile is the client and that they are the sole resource for safety. They believe that helping that exile involves moving mountains. That it would take an army, a trainload of equipment, and a magic wand! They wonder how there could be any help from inside this bereft system because they have no sense of the Self, no access to their lifeboat. Yet being heard and feeling validated is just the evidence managers and firefighters need that the Self exists. If the Self can accept and hold them in positive regard, they feel reassured that it can do the same for wounded exiles.

BACKLASH

Sometimes a piece of sensitive work will activate protective parts who are very accustomed to running the show. In what we call *backlash*, they get back in the driver's seat and find ways to distance the client from their recent exposure to wounded parts and memories of bad experiences. Backlash happens when protectors are still scared of returning to the exile's story and being overwhelmed by its feelings. It can also occur when an exile feels desperately let down because the client made a promise and didn't follow through.

It's important to understand that backlash will happen with all clients and with any kind of addictive process. Typically, it involves a familiar set of protective parts taking over. For example, firefighters might ignite a craving and lure the client in the direction of pills, gambling, or pornography. Managers might then weigh in, berating the client and criticizing everything they do (or don't do) as wrong. This inner polarity unsettles exiles, igniting their shamefulness and hopelessness. It makes clients worry that they can't change or that their parts won't let them change. But backlash is part of the process. Our job is to stay calm, reassuring, and optimistic.

As we help the client identify this addictive cycle, we interview protectors to discover what they feared would happen if they didn't take over, which helps them unblend. As they reconnect with the Self, they remember they're not alone and don't have to solve all client's problems. At the same time, we ask the client if they noticed any of their exiles during the week. If so, we make a plan for those parts to go to a safe place between sessions if they're willing, and we encourage the client to check in on them if protectors permit. If not, the client can promise to return at a later date, and it's our job to remember to return to that part in the next session.

Here is an example of how we attend to backlash. Janette was a twenty-seven-year-old, single, nonbinary Jamaican who came to the United States with their parents and two younger brothers when they were ten years old. Their mother abused prescription drugs and their father was rarely home—Janette's mother told them he was living with another woman—which left Janette feeling responsible for their younger brothers. They got excellent grades in school, and they were now a whiz at their social services agency job, but they spent many evenings bingeing, purging, and sometimes slicing their arms and legs with tiny cuts.

ATTENDING TO BACKLASH

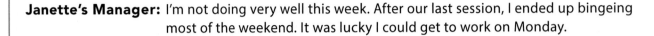

Janette's Manager: I'm not doing very well this week. After our last session, I ended up bingeing most of the weekend. It was lucky I could get to work on Monday.

Therapist: Oh, I am sorry you had such a rough time of it!

Janette's Manager: I haven't been that bad in a while.

Therapist: Shall we get in touch with the bingeing part to see if we can get you some relief?

Janette's Manager: Well, we can try.

Therapist: Can you see the bingeing part?

Janette's Manager: I see it eating. It's sickening.

Therapist: Sounds like another part doesn't like the bingeing. Will it step back for now and trust you to help it?

Janette's Manager: I guess it will step back for now, but it still hates all that.

Therapist: It can just watch you for now and see how this goes. How do you feel toward the bingeing part now?

Janette: Okay.

Therapist: It's okay to be curious? (*Janette nods.*) What does the bingeing part want to show you about last weekend?

Janette: This part says it just wanted to eat. It knows I really like sweets, and it doesn't care what happens.

Therapist: What would happen if this part didn't get you the sweets?

Janette: It says I never get anything I want.

Therapist: What is that like for you?

Janette: I work long hours and then just come back to my little apartment. And last week, we were talking about the time my mother passed out at home. I had to call 911 for her, and my brothers went with me to the hospital and freaked out, and… that was bad.

Therapist: I remember. You had to take care of everyone, and your mom was very sick. You did not have anything good or sweet in your life. If you and I could help that burdened teenage part, would the bingeing part be able to take a break sometimes?

Janette: Yes, the teenage part needs help.

Therapist: Of course it does. Let's check in with it now. Do you see it? (*Janette nods.*) Does it see you? You are here for this part. What does it need right now?

Janette: The teenage part wants to get out of there, but it can't leave.

Therapist: Would it like us to come back and help it leave?

Janette: Yes.

Therapist: Okay. Tell the bingeing part that you can help the burdened teenager. The connection won't always be perfect. Last week, you two lost touch, and the binger stepped in to help. But you're on it again. You can get the teenager out of there when it is ready.

When exiles finally connect with the client's Self, their communications regarding past events may continue into the days following a session, evoking strong negative feelings about time and opportunities lost. If these feelings frighten protectors and they don't trust the Self sufficiently, they will take steps to banish the exile once again. As a result, the client who promises to pay attention during the week is not always able to follow through, as occurred with Janette as they lost touch with their burdened teenage part. If a client does promise attention to an exile and fails to give it, repair (sometimes with a good dose of patience) is in order and is effective. You can also help prevent backlash between sessions by using any of the following intervention options.

Intervention Options for Exiles Between Sessions

First, check on potential interference. Does any part object to the client staying connected with the exile during the week? If so, simply put the exile in a safe place of its choosing and return in the next session. If not, try one or more of the following actions.

Safe Place:

- Invite the exile to move to a place it associates with healing.

- Invite the exile to be in the present with the client.

- Invite a benign protector (e.g., a loving older sibling part) to stay with the exile until the next session.

- Take the exile to a safe place with a beloved pet.

Actions:

- If protectors will allow, have the client write a short note to the exile each morning or night.

- Invite the client to find a symbol of the exile (e.g., photo, small figurine) to keep in their purse, backpack, or pocket.

- When an exiled memory comes up, prompt the client to visualize the exile in a new safe space.

- Have the client ask the exile not to blend until the client has the support of a friend, a group, or their therapist.

- Invite the client to send the exile a golden thread* from their heart to the exile's heart, or from their heart to the exile's hand.

- Encourage the client to send the exile a soft, soothing, and calming breath.

- Have the client ask the exile to share just one important thing until the client has time to return and hear more.

- Ask the client to reassure the exile that it can stay home when they go to school or work.

- Prompt the client to update the exile on their current age.

- Invite the client to show the exile other parts who have unburdened and feel better.

---

* Thanks to Michi Rose for the golden thread exercise.

RECOVERY AND RECURRENCE

When clients are released from an inpatient treatment center, or they are working on their changing their addictive patterns with the help of outpatient therapy, they are fragile and emotionally vulnerable. They face interpersonal and work challenges without their drug or practice of choice. They generally feel alone, are grieving past losses, and still crave relief. This is a moment when another firefighter might step in to pinch-hit—for example, by bingeing and purging instead of drinking—or when the client might just return to their preferred addictive process. The protective system activates in response to exiled vulnerability coming back into consciousness. This is known as a *recurrence* (we prefer the term to relapse, which is shaming), and it causes the psyche to ignite with familiar suffering. One over-excited part ricochets off the next in a scrum of self-disgust, self-loathing, fury, and fear (*Maybe I can't get better!*).

Traditional treatment often questions the client's intentions (*Do you even want to get better?*), blames them for recurring symptoms (*How many meetings have you attended? Have you reached out to your sponsor lately?*), and employs strong directives (*Just resist that craving!*) in the belief that this will help the client regain control. While a sense of imperative about helping the client get back on track is understandable, this approach is unlikely to be helpful. If we weigh in at this point from the perspective of a worried, advice-giving manager, we are making the mistake of pressing a thumb on the manager side of the scale. So, in IFS, we do something different. Rather than helping the client get back in control, we guide them to stay in close contact with their recently deposed firefighters and get back into relationship.

We remain positive, compassionate, and most of all, calm. Our job is to convey confidence that we can get to the bottom of how this started and what keeps it going. Our assurance is essential. We listen, knowing the client will feel better when their Self reconnects with their protectors and has access to their exiles. We assure clients that new Self-to-part patterns are empowering and they're not back at square one. We remind them that all this is very predictable. Recurrence is similar to backlash and is a normal aspect of the healing process. We remind the client that cutting back or being sober could release a surge of painful memories, older and more recent. We caution that critics might respond with shaming and that, in response, firefighters would step up with the usual temptations. We remind the client that the addictive process is a cycle with its own rationale and its own aims. It does make sense.

Now that the cycle is back in action, we can name the parts and ask them to slow down. We don't work on improving protector behavior; we work on improving the client's ability to reach out to protectors, understand their motives, and build attachment. We help them see that their compulsive parts, who believe the client is a vulnerable child who needs relief, are making choices. In this way, we move clients from confusion to clarity. With their new perspective on using, clients can see that their firefighter parts aren't just crazy and destructive, they are opting to survive. Recurrence is thus another opportunity to calm protectors and proceed with the project of connecting with exiles. This approach is affirming and optimistic. We find that most clients can be curious about why they are using again. They can also make use of new practices to rebalance emotionally.

An Intervention Option after Recurrence

This exercise is intended to help the client step back from fear and self-condemnation and understand why their parts are once again using a substance or engaging in a compulsive practice in a problematic way. Here we address a blended system and ask protective parts to step back and trust us. A sample script is provided for you throughout, as well as some guiding prompts to walk you through each step of the intervention.

1. Remind the client that the addictive cycle makes sense and that by inquiring together, you can get to the bottom of the most recent recurrence.

   When protective parts get worried, they fall back on the old tactics they trust. Firefighter parts might begin drinking, gambling, bingeing, using drugs, or engaging in any other compulsive behavior that aims to soothe or distract. In turn, manager parts might step in with shaming or expressions of disgust. This is normal and predictable. When this happens, we can ask firefighter parts about their intentions. They generally say they're worried that exiles will overwhelm the system with painful emotions, old memories, or untold secrets. In this exercise, we will invite them to explain their reasons. If a compulsive behavior alarmed any other parts, we can help those parts too.

2. When the connection between the client and therapist is firm, guide the client to invite their protective parts to a meeting.

   Let's have a summit meeting. Let's invite all the parts who need to be here right now to join us. Invite the compulsive firefighter parts and the critical manager parts to come sit at a big table with you. They are all welcome. Who needs your attention first?

3. Hear from whatever part needs the client's attention first. For example, a critical manager might share about their fear of chaos and emotional overwhelm. A stirred-up firefighter might discuss their fears of exile overwhelm and managerial shaming. Either way, reassure the part that you are here to listen.

   We are not here to control or criticize you. We want to understand your intentions. What are you concerned about? How were you trying to help?

- If a firefighter is reacting to a manager:

  If we could help that manager part stop controlling or caretaking or overworking, would you need to _____ (use substances, gamble, overeat, watch pornography, etc.) in the same way?

- If a manager part is reacting to a firefighter:

  If we could help that using part so it would _____ (keep its agreements, find a more benign way to distract, etc.), would you need to keep attacking it?

- If either protective part is afraid of an exile:

  If you saw there was a safe way for that injured part to feel wanted and loved, would you be willing to downshift a bit?

4. Ask both protector teams to let the client's Self help the exile they protect (it may be the same exile or different exiles). When they agree, welcome the exile by beginning with a one-way Self-to-part bid for connection.

   Let that hurt young part know that you are here, that you are paying attention. Let it know that it's not alone. How does it respond?

5. If the Self and the exile connect and protectors are still supportive, continue with a two-way connection and witness the exile.

   What does this part want you to know? What caused its hurt, loneliness, or sense of shame? Are you taking this in? Let it know. Can it feel your concern and care? How does it respond?

6. When this feels complete, clarify the cycle of disconnection by inviting the client to draw and discuss their addiction triangle. Which protectors react to each other? Which exiled part(s) get triggered? Does this feel familiar or new? Then draw and discuss another triangle that depicts what happens when the client's Self is in the lead.

   Do the parts feel connected to you now? What do they need from you to keep toning down? Thank them for taking the risk of being with you today. Do they want homework or a set plan to work on before next session?

Conclusion

In IFS, we offer our clients hope. We normalize having many parts, many opinions, and sometimes lots of mental conflict. And we assert that Self-leadership is possible even when consensus isn't. Their protectors are polarized over how to handle vulnerability and emotional pain. Like embattled siblings, they have no idea how to resolve their differences. Accordingly, we assert that each has validity and guide the client to listen to both points of view. We don't ask clients to get in control; we show them how to get in connection. At the same time, we ask the parts to notice the client's Self. Here it is, available and nonjudgmental. What if the Self could help? This discussion may take a whole clinical hour or more. If it does, there is no need to worry. Our clients don't need to be somewhere forward in time—they need to be right here.

Our job is to make all parts welcome. In therapy, this is a special invitation to the ones who are unbearably afraid, ashamed, angry, or compulsive. We know our clients have the resources to help these parts. We show them how to access those resources. Ultimately, we guide them to explore their vision for the addictive behavior in the future, set their own goals, and provide their own definition of sobriety. We can say with confidence that many clients will like this approach, most will be relieved to meet their parts, and all will have the capacity for compassion and inner leadership. We've shown you how it can be done. We hope we've inspired you to give it a try.

References

For your convenience, purchasers of the book can download a PDF version of the exercises and handouts at pesipublishing.com/addictions

Chödrön, P. (2007). *The places that scare you: A guide to fearlessness in difficult times.* Shambhala Press.

Felitti, V. J. (2004). *The origins of addiction: Evidence from The Adverse Childhood Experience Study.* Department of Preventive Medicine, Kaiser Permanente.

Felitti, V. J., Anda, R. F., Nordenberg, D., Williamson, D. F., Spitz, A. M., Edwards, V., Koss, M. P., & Marks, J. S. (1998). Relationship of childhood abuse and household dysfunction to many of the leading causes of death in adults: The Adverse Childhood Experiences (ACE) Study. *American Journal of Preventive Medicine, 14*(4), 245–258.

Hari, J. (2015). *Chasing the scream: The first and last days of the war on drugs.* Bloomsbury Publishing.

Hart, C. L. (2021). *Drug use for grown-ups: Chasing liberty in the land of fear.* Penguin.

Interlandi, J. (2022, June 24). Experts say we have the tools to fight addiction. So why are more Americans overdosing than ever? *The New York Times.* https://www.nytimes.com/2022/06/24/opinion/addiction-overdose-mental-health.html?smid=em-share

Lewis, M. (2015). *The biology of desire: Why addiction is not a disease.* Public Affairs Books.

Menakem, R. (2017). *My grandmother's hands: Racialized trauma and the pathway to mending our hearts and bodies.* Central Recovery Press.

Miller, W. R., & Rollnick, S. (2013). *Motivational interviewing: Helping people change* (3rd ed.). Guilford Press.

Redfern, E. E. (2022). *Internal family systems therapy: Supervision and consultation.* Routledge.

Schwartz, R. C. (2016). Perpetrator parts. In M. Sweezy & E. L. Ziskind (Eds.), *Innovations and elaborations in internal family systems therapy* (pp. 109–122). Routledge.

Schwartz, R. C., & Sweezy, M. (2020). *Internal family systems therapy* (2nd ed.). Guilford Press.

Sykes, C. (2016). An IFS lens on addiction: Compassion for extreme parts. In M. Sweezy & E. L. Ziskind (Eds.), *Innovations and elaborations in internal family systems therapy* (pp. 29–48). Routledge.

Szalavitz, M. (2016). *Unbroken brain: A revolutionary new way of understanding addiction.* St. Martin's Press.

Tatarsky, A. (Ed.) (2007). *Harm reduction psychotherapy: A new treatment for drug and alcohol problems.* Jason Aronson, Inc.